Ketogenic Diet

The Complete Ketogenic Diet Cookbook For Beginners - Delicious Recipes To Shed Weight, Heal Your Body, and Regain Confidence

Table of Contents

Introduction

The foods and nutrients we chose to put in our bodies have a direct impact on our health. This includes both the short term with our ability to ward off illness and infection, as well as long term as we age and face other health challenges.

If we eat primarily healthy foods, we will increase our chances of keeping our bodies healthy. Conversely, if we make poor choices and take in unhealthy foods, or foods that do not complement our individual physiological needs, we increase our chances of getting sick. In fact, eating a healthy diet can help reduce the risk of a number of diseases and conditions, including type 2 diabetes, osteoporosis, heart disease, stroke and some forms of cancer. In fact, a healthy diet even impacts your dental health, promoting strong teeth and gums and preventing tooth decay.

Of course, every body is different and each individual is impacted by genetics and other environmental factors. Consequently, there are a multitude of diet plans available. One eating plan may work for your sibling, but not work for you.

In this book, we will be discussing the Ketogenic Diet, which has three primary components: low carbs, medium proteins and high fat. As with any change in diet or exercise, please speak with your physician first to make sure this is appropriate for your needs.

The Ketogenic Diet

What Is The Ketogenic Diet?

With decades of use under its belt, the Ketogenic Diet, also simply known as the Keto Diet, is a tried and true method for healthy eating and weight loss.

Historically, the Keto Diet was embraced in the 1920s and 30s as a treatment for epilepsy as an alternative to traditional fasting, which was a long-accepted practice for controlling seizures. Additionally, this diet was used to help control diabetes in patient. However, as different medications and methods were discovered, the Ketogenic Diet was abandoned and relatively forgotten for decades.

The Ketogenic Diet focuses on low carbohydrate, medium protein and high fat intake. There are several different adaptations of this diet but for general purposes, the daily calories are comprised of 2% to 5% of carbs, between 6% to 20% of protein and 75% to 90% of fat.

The number of carbohydrates you take in is important, because your body turns them into glucose and insulin. Glucose is easier for your body to process into energy than fat, so if you have both glucose and fat in your body, it's going to take the glucose first and tuck the fat away later if its needed.

With this in mind, the Ketogenic Diet flips that process on its head by severely minimizing the carbs introduced into the body. Thus, the body will use the fat to turn into energy.

This puts the body into a state of ketosis, which is a survival state. However, with the Ketogenic Diet, one is not starving the body of necessary calories, but of unnecessary carbs.

How Can It Benefit You?

A low carbohydrate diet is widely accepted as a beneficial approach to both weight loss and of eating healthy. While the Ketogenic Diet has been used for nearly a century, other forms of low-carb diets have underscored the importance of this approach.

For example, the popular Atkins Diet, which has gained increasing attention since the 1970s, has a heavy emphasis on a reducing carbs. In fact, the traditional form of the Atkins Diet includes two weeks of stringent adherence to an extremely low carb, ketogenic phase.

Studies have suggested following a carbohydrate-restrictive diet is beneficial for people who have, or are at risk of, type 2 diabetes and may have long term benefits for people who have other neurological disorders, such as multiple sclerosis, autism, Parkinson's disease and Alzheimer's.

On a long term basis, a diet such as the Ketogenic Diet often results in fast weight loss, since it launches the body into that state of ketosis, and zeroes in on fats as the primary source of converting calories into energy.

Since carbs are severely restricted, the Ketogenic Diet compensates by relaxing on proteins, but especially fats. While some find it difficult to follow on a long-term basis and want to return to a more 'Americanized' diet—which is often comprised of as much as 50% of protein—the allowance of fats can compensate.

While the body is burning fat, it's important to keep in mind that there are many different areas where fat is stored. The primary regions are subcutaneous, which is under the skin, and visceral, which is located in the abdominal cavity. That visceral fat often tucks itself around organs, which can lead to unhealthy inflammation.

Additionally, excess visceral fat can lead to insulin resistance; dangerous because healthy insulin levels regulate normal metabolism of both carbs and fats.

So, while the Ketogenic Diet leans toward a heavier proportion of fat intake, this actually helps burn fats faster than a diet that allows more carbohydrates.

If you're looking at cholesterols, the practice of the Ketogenic Diet to consume fat can actually increase high-density lipoproteins (HDL)... also known as the 'good cholesterol.' That good cholesterol, or HDL, is commonly known to go hand in hand with lowering the risk of heart disease.

Diets that eliminate carbohydrates, such as the Ketogenic Diet, has been identified as a good way to reduce blood pressure, which is a risk factor for diseases such as stroke, heart disease and kidney failure, as well as many other diseases.

In all, a low carb diet, while very restrictive in some respects, enables people to take control of one of the greatest adversaries in a healthy diet: the carbohydrate.

Foods To Avoid? Foods To Eat?

So, we've talked about the science-y components of the Ketogenic Diet. That's all good and fine but chances are this is what it comes down to... what can you eat on the Ketogenic Diet, and what do you need to avoid?

Let's start with the positives. What CAN you eat?

First, there are the fats and oils, which make up the largest portion of the diet plan. Think of these as the building blocks of your meal. The foundation. Frankly, they are what make the other foods taste yummy. Fats flavor and help hold in the moisture of your other foods.

Fats are broken down into a couple different combinations:
1. **Saturated fats**. Ketogenic Diet approved. Examples of saturated fats include: butter, lard, coconut oil and ghee. Other foods rich in saturated fats are beef, lamb, pork, poultry with skin and cheese.

2. **Monounsaturated fats.** Ketogenic Diet approved. These can help reduce bad cholesterol levels, thus lowering your risk for heart disease and stroke. As a rule of thumb, oils with monounsaturated fats are in a liquid state at room temperature but then turn to a solid when the temperature drops.
   Oils high in monounsaturated fats are olive, peanut, canola and sesame oils.
   Other foods high in monounsaturated fats are avocadoes and peanut butter, as well as various nuts and seeds.

3. **Polyunsaturated Fats.** Within the Ketogenic Diet, naturally-occurring fats in this category are okay. In fact, they contain essential fats that your body cannot produce, such as omega-3 and omega-6 fatty acids. Naturally-occurring Polyunsaturated Fats include fatty fishes, such as salmon.

Conversely, there are Polyunsaturated Fats that are not naturally occurring, such as margarines. These foods should be avoided.

4. **Trans Fats.** These should be avoided at all costs. Trans fats are fats that ahave been undergone a chemical change to extend their shelf live. Remember that good cholesterol, the HDL? Trans fats lower HDLs, while raising LDLs... or the bad cholesterol.
   Trans fats are sneaky, and hide in foods such as preprocessed baked goods and other snacks. However, in the past few years, trans fats have been given the black eye they deserve, and many processed foods now tout a 'trans fat free' label.

So again, while fats in general are Ketogenic Diet approved, this doesn't give a consumer carte blanche when it comes to fats. Keep your awareness high to determine what fats are and are not okay.

Also on the approved list is a moderate portion of **proteins**. Proteins can include beef, pork and chicken products, as well as eggs and almond butter. A huge plus in most people's opinion is that bacon is okay on the Ketogenic Diet, providing it does not contain extra fillers or has an excessive amount of sugar. And as we all know, everything is better with bacon.

Next up is **dairy**, which should only be a moderate part of your diet. When selecting dairy items, it's best to go with organic and raw products, since fillers generally have higher amounts of carbohydrates than unprocessed counterparts. Also, lean toward full fat products versus low fat or fat free, as the lower fat items also have fillers which add to the carbs.

While thinking about the next food group, it's time to separate the **fruits and vegetables**, which often go hand in hand. For a Ketogenic Diet, vegetables are encouraged, but fruits should be added sparingly because they are high in sugar. Large fruits, such as bananas have the highest sugar content so should be completely avoided. When selecting vegetables, the focus should be on leafy vegetables, such as kale and spinach, as well as broccoli. These foods have lower carbs and sugar. Root vegetables should be used sparingly, because they have higher sugar content. However, those vegetables, such as onions, garlic and turnip, are great for adding flavor to soups. Because of their high starch content, potatoes should be avoided.

Like dairy products, **nuts and seeds** are approved in the Ketogenic Diet in small amounts. While they are high in fats, their carbohydrate content can add up quickly. Some of the lower carb nuts include pecans and macadamia nuts, while nuts such as pistachios and cashews should be omitted because they are very high in carbs.

Of course, **beverages** run the gamut of good versus bad but people on the Ketogenic Diet need to make sure they are keeping hydrated because the foods that are critical this diet also have a diuretic effect. In fact, dehydration is so prevalent that the term 'Keto Flu' has been coined, describing the condition that many people who just start the diet experience. Symptoms include headache, fatigue, cramps, etc. To combat this, drink plenty of water and replenish electrolytes by drinking bone broths and sports drinks with Stevia or sucralose.

A minimum of eight glasses of water is recommended daily. Other approved beverages are coffee and teas and unsweetened coconut or almond milk. Diet sodas should be avoided and alcohol should be consumed sparingly, if at all.

Finally are **spices and condiments**. These are an essential part of food preparation, but some items, particularly processed items such as ketchup and other sauces, have higher carbohydrate counts. There are lower carb alternatives, so keep an eye out for these in the grocery store, and use them, but still sparingly.

Salt and pepper are approved and while there are carbs in spices, they are generally used sparingly in cooking, so they won't throw off your carb count too much.

As you can see, there is a variety of foods that are okay on the Ketogenic Diet. What should you avoid?

Grains should be avoided on the Ketogenic Diet. These include breads, rice, corn and pastas. It also includes whole grains, such as wheat, barley and quinoa. Sugar is often snuck into processed foods. Since sugars should be avoided, a good rule of thumb is to steer clear of items such as soda, ice cream and other processed foods. While dieters often gravitate to low fat or fat free alternatives, these items often contain fillers. Stick with full fat products.

Starches should be avoided, and include oats and items such as muesli. Starchy vegetables, like yams, sweet potatoes and potatoes, should also be removed from your diet. As mentioned earlier, trans fats are simply bad for your body and should be avoided.

Foods to eat liberally:

Vegetables:
- Spinach
- Kale
- Chives
- Lettuce
- Bok choy
- Swiss chard
- Celery
- Summer squash (including zucchini)
- Cucumber
- Asparagus

Fruits:
- Avocados

Protein:
- Grass-fed meats (beef, venison, lamb)
- Grass-fed offals (liver, kidney, other organ meats)
- Wild-harvested fish
- Wild-harvested seafood
- Pork
- Poultry
- Eggs
- Butter
- Ghee

Fats:
- Lard
- Chicken Fat
- Tallow
- Coconut oil
- Olive oil

Beverages:
- Water
- Coffee
- Tea

Sides and Condiments:
- Mayonnaise
- Mustard

- Spices
- Herbs
- Lemon/lime juice and zest
- Pesto
- Pickles
- Homemade bone broth
- Pork rinds (great for a breading alternative)

Foods to eat in moderate amounts:
Vegetables:
- Cabbage
- Brussels sprouts
- Squash
- Peppers
- Tomatoes
- Turnip
- Rutabaga
- Cauliflower
- Peas
- Artichokes
- Mushrooms
- Garlic

Fruits:
- Coconut
- Berries
- Rhubarb

Protein:
- Grain-fed meats (beef, venison, lamb)
- Grain-fed offals (liver, kidney, other organ meats)
- Farm-raised fish
- Bacon

Full Fat Dairy Products:
- Yogurt
- Cottage Cheese
- Cheese
- Sour Cream

Nuts & Seeds:
- Macadamia nuts
- Pecans
- Almonds
- Pine nuts
- Flaxseed
- Sesame Seeds
- Sunflower Seeds
- Hemp Seeds
- Walnuts

Beverages:
- Dry red wine
- Dry white wine
- Spirits

Foods to avoid:
Grains:
- Wheat
- Rye
- Rice
- Corn
- Barley
- Baked goods

Vegetables:
Potatoes
Sweet potatoes

Fruit and juices:
- Papaya
- Mango
- Banana
- Grapes

Others:
- Cow milk
- Processed foods
- Refined fats
- Artificial sweeteners

This list is far from comprehensive, but it is a good starting point for what to look for and what to avoid!

Ketgenic FAQs

As with any diet, there are a number of questions that arise, both on the outset and later during the process. Here are some of the most frequently asked questions.

Q: What is ketosis?
A: Ketosis is the normal state your body is in when it starts burning fat, versus glucose for energy. In the Ketogenic Diet, the key is to limit carbs that turn into glucose and insulin. Since the body naturally wants to burn glucose, if both glucose and fat is available, the body will store the fat for later and instead use glucose. However, when it turns fat into energy (also known as ketones), you are in the desired state of ketosis.

Q: How long does it take to get into the state of ketosis?
A: When starting the Ketogenic Diet, it generally takes several days for your body to adjust and go into ketosis. Depending on a number of factors—food intake, body type and exercise—it can take as little as 2 to as much as 7 days to enter this state.

Q: How do I know when I am in ketosis?
A: The simplest way to track ketosis is by purchasing urine strips at your local pharmacy to measure the ketones your body is producing. These will not give you a concluding: "You are in ketosis" statement, but they will show your ketone production.

Q: Why is drinking water important?
A: The foods used in the Ketogenic Diet have a diuretic effect, so it is important to replenish the water that is being lost to avoid side effects. A minimum of 8 glasses of water should be taken in every day; the more, the better.

Q: What is the Keto Flu?
A: The term 'Keto Flu' describes the condition that many people experience who just begin the Ketogenic Diet. Symptoms include headache, fatigue, cramps, etc. To avoid or combat this, keep yourself hydrated. Drink plenty of water (a minimum of 8 glasses per day) and replenish electrolytes by drinking bone broths and sports drinks with Stevia or sucralose.

Q: Is ketosis dangerous?
A: No. Ketosis is a natural state. When you are in proper ketosis, by following a Ketogenic Diet, you are not starving your body. By reducing carbs, which in part turns to glucose, you are forcing your body to burn fat, since glucose is not readily available.

Q: Can I add too much fat in this diet?

A: Yes. There are a number of different types of fat, as explained in the previous section. Plus, in order to lose weight, we need to burn off more calories than we take in, and too much fat adds calories. When adding fat to your diet, be aware of what are good and bad fats, and add the good ones... but don't sit down with a lard pie.

Q: What are macros?

A: Macros is short for macronutrients, which are fats, carbs and proteins. It's important to track these macros, particularly in the beginning of the diet, so you are aware of what may or may not be helping you achieve ketosis, and lose weight.

Q: How can I track my macros?

A: There are a number of apps and links to helping you track your macros. The Ketogenic Calculator available through ruled.me is a great example of one.

Q: Will increasing my fat intake result in high cholesterol?

A: On a low carb diet, such as the Ketogenic Diet, evidence suggests that it is effective for weight loss and reducing cardiovascular risk factors, such as high cholesterol. Also, consuming fat can actually increase high-density lipoproteins (HDL). That good cholesterol, or HDL, is commonly known to go hand in hand with lowering the risk of heart disease.

Q: Why can't I have artificial sweeteners?

A: Artificial sweeteners are chemicals, and are known to disrupt the state of ketosis. Besides disrupting the desired result in this diet, it's just a bad idea to introduce chemicals into your body. However, natural sweeteners, such as Stevia, are approved for use in this diet.

Q: Will this diet make me tired?

A: Fatigue is an indicator that you are not in full ketosis. This is often evident when people begin the Ketogenic Diet, or if they are not balancing their diet successfully. Take note of your fat intake, and drink plenty of water. Any feeling of tiredness should pass within a few days of starting this diet.

Q: So, I don't have to count calories with this diet, right?

A: While the Ketogenic Diet is not about counting calories, but noting macros instead, it is still important to be aware of the calories you are taking in. Some 'approved' foods have higher calorie content than others A simple rule of thumb is, if you take in more calories than you burn off in a day, you will gain weight.

Q: Can I still exercise with this diet?
A: Aerobic exercise (running, biking, treadmill exercise, etc) is not impacted by the Ketogenic Diet. If you are lifting weights, there are modified Ketogenic Diet plans that help you take in enough carbs to help muscle recovery.

Tips for Eating Out

When people start on a diet, one significant concern is: "Can I still go out to eat occasionally?" Because, let's face it, a restaurant might offer guidelines on their menu for items, such as vegan, gluten free or vegetarian items, but they generally do not cater to a specific diet.

So, do you avoid eating out and avoid the social scene altogether? Absolutely not. We'll share with you some tips on how to dine out and still stick to your diet.

First, **plan** your dining experience.

What are you craving? Are you in the mood for a burger or baked haddock? There are some restaurant types that would be best to avoid, such as pizza houses or Italian restaurants. However, restaurant owners are becoming increasingly aware of dietary restrictions and often accommodate special requests, such as wrapping a burger in lettuce instead of in a bun, or turning a sandwich into a salad by taking the basic ingredients and incorporating them in a salad instead of served in a bun.

Steakhouses and seafood restaurants are good options to help you stick to your Ketogenic Diet. Also those in the Greek, Middle Eastern and Mediterranean niches will have healthy options, as will Asian restaurants.

Frankly, even fast food joints offer healthier choices nowadays.

If you know what restaurant you are going to be eating at, **look at the menu** online. If the restaurant doesn't have an official menu page that you can pursue before going out, you may be able to find the menu on its social media page. There are also independent menu websites, like menupix.com where restaurants can link to their menu and readers can actually upload pictures that they took of the most current menu.

After you locate the menu, select the keto-friendly option you will order ahead of time. If there are couple different options, make a mental note to ask your server about recommendations and ingredients when you get there.

Next, have a **snack** before you leave. If you go to a restaurant feeling ravenous, you are more likely to make an unhealthy diet decision, like having a warm piece of bread before your meal comes. Or being tempted by that breaded, fried haddock instead of opting for its baked, uncoated cousin.

Drink plenty of water, which will help give you the sensation of being full. If ice water slows you down, ask your server for water without ice, or a bottled water option.

Before ordering, **ask questions**. Remember, this is your meal, and you are paying good money for it, so you deserve to have your questions answered. Plus, your server is instructed to help you as necessary, so don't be afraid to ask questions like: Is that breaded? Can I substitute a vegetable for the starch? Can I have my dressing on the side?

Another important question to ask is if a dish is prepared with a sauce, which is often packed with sugars, thickened with cornstarch, or contain additives such as MSG.

Finally, **don't stress** about the meal. You're eating out to be with friends, or for the convenience when you aren't able to cook at home. If you eat a little breading, some sauce, it's okay. It happens. Enjoy yourself, enjoy your companions and enjoy your meal!

Keto Diet Recipes

Smoothies & Breakfast

Basic Green Smoothie

Serves: 2
Preparation time: 5 minutes

Ingredients:
- ½ European cucumber
- Juice of ½ lemon
- 1 avocado, ripe
- 4 ½ cup kale
- 1 ¾ cup water

Instructions:
1. Combine all ingredients, except kale, in your blender.
2. Add kale on the very top, then add water.
3. Blend and enjoy!

Sleep In Smoothie

Serves: 1
Preparation time: 5 minutes

Ingredients:

- 1 egg, raw, pasteurized
- 2/3 cup almond milk
- 1 cup blueberries
- 2 cup spinach, raw
- ½ avocado, ripe

Instructions:

1. Combine all ingredients in your blender.
2. Blend and enjoy.

Keto Tropical Smoothie

Serves 1
Preparation time: 5 minutes

Ingredients:

- 6 or 7 ice cubes
- 2/3 cup coconut milk
- 1/3 cup cream
- 2 Tbsp. flaxseed meal
- 1 Tbsp. coconut oil
- 18-20 drops liquid Stevia, depending on desire for sweetness
- 1 tsp. mango extract
- ½ tsp. blueberry extract
- ½ tsp. banana extract

Instructions:

1. Combine all ingredients in your blender.
2. Wait a few minutes for the flaxseed to absorb the liquid.
3. Blend and enjoy.

Easy Strawberry Smoothie

Serves 5
Preparation time: 5 minutes

Ingredients:

- 2 cup strawberries, frozen
- 1 ¾ cup almond milk, unsweetened
- 1 avocado
- ¼ cup Erythritol or other sweetener

Instructions:

1. Combine all ingredients in your blender.
2. Blend and enjoy.

Vanilla Smoothie

Serves 1
Preparation time: 5 minutes

Ingredients:

- 2 egg yolks, pasteurized
- 2/3 cup mascarpone cheese or creamed coconut milk
- 1/3 cup water
- 5 ice cubes
- 1 Tbsp. coconut oil
- ½ tsp. vanilla extract
- 3-4 drops liquid Stevia

Instructions:

1. Combine all ingredients in your blender.
2. Blend and enjoy.

Healthy Shamrock Shake

Serves 1

Preparation time: 5 minutes

Ingredients:

- 2/3 cup ricotta cheese (whole milk)
- ¼ cup half and half
- 2 egg yolks, pasteurized
- 2/3 cup spinach, fresh
- ¼ tsp. vanilla extract
- ½ tsp. peppermint extract
- 2 Tbsp. Stevia or other sweetener
- 1 cup ice, crushed

Instructions:

1. Combine all ingredients in your blender.
2. Blend and enjoy.

Creamy Cinnamon Smoothie

Serves: 1
Preparation time: 5 minutes

Ingredients:

- 2/3 cup almond milk
- 1/3 cup vanilla whey protein
- 1 Tbsp. chia seeds
- ¼ tsp. cinnamon
- 1 Tbsp. coconut oil, extra virgin
- 2/3 cup water
- 2-3 ice cubes

Instructions:

1. Combine all ingredients in your blender.
2. Blend and enjoy.

Coconut Cherry Vanilla Smoothie

Serves 1

Preparation time: 5 minutes

Ingredients:
- ¼ cup coconut milk, canned
- 6-7 ice cubes
- 2/3 cup water
- 1/8 tsp. vanilla powder
- Sprinkle of sea salt
- ¼ cup sweet cherries, frozen

Instructions
1. Combine all ingredients in your blender.
2. Blend and enjoy.

Key Lime Smoothie Bowl

Servings: 1 to 2
Preparation time: 5 minutes

Ingredients:

- ½ avocado
- 2/3 cup coconut milk
- 1 cup spinach, raw
- 2 Tbsp. lime juice
- Lime zest
- 1 tsp. vanilla extract
- 2 Tbsp. honey

Toppings (if desired):

- 2 Tbsp. coconut
- 2-3 Tbsp. pomegranate arils
- ½ cup kiwi, sliced

Instructions:

1. Combine all ingredients in your blender.
2. Blend.
3. Garnish with toppings and enjoy.

Cauliflower Fritters

Serves: 6 fritters
Preparation time: 10 minutes
Cooking time: 15 minutes

Ingredients:

- 1 head cauliflower
- 2 eggs, large
- 2/3 cup almond flour
- 1 Tbsp. + 1 tsp. nutritional yeast
- ½ tsp. turmeric
- Sea salt, to taste
- Black pepper, to taste
- 2-3 Tbsp. ghee

Instructions:

1. Break cauliflower into florets. Place them into a large pot, cover in water and boil for 8 minutes. Strain. Transfer the cauliflower to a food processor and pulse until it's a rice consistency.
2. Combine all ingredients except ghee in a mixing bowl. Stir well. Create patties with the mixture.
3. On a skillet, heat ghee over medium heat. Place 3 patties in the pan and cook until golden brown, flipping after 3 or 4 minutes. Repeat with the rest.
4. Serve hot.

Scrambled Egg with Smoked Salmon

Serves 2
Preparation time: 5 minutes
Cooking time: 5 minutes

Ingredients:
- 6 eggs, large
- 1 tsp. seasoning
- 3-4 oz. smoked salmon
- 1 Tbsp. shallots, sliced
- 2 Tbsp. capers

Instructions:
1. Combine eggs and seasoning.
2. Cook over low heat.
3. When ready, top with salmon, shallots and capers and serve.

Bacon Spinach Frittata

Bacon Spinach Frittata
Serves: 6
Preparation time: 5 minutes
Cooking time: 20 minutes

Ingredients:
- 5-6 strips bacon
- 1 cup almond or coconut milk
- 8 eggs, large
- 4 egg whites, large
- 1/8 cup onion, diced
- ¾ cup grape tomatoes, quartered
- 2 ¼ cup spinach, raw

Instructions:
1. Preheat oven to 400 degrees (F).
2. In a cast iron pan, cook the bacon over medium heat. Cool and crumble the bacon. Reserve bacon grease.
3. Whisk milk, eggs, and egg whites in a bowl. Set aside.
4. Sauté onions in bacon grease for 3 minutes, or until opaque. Add the tomato and spinach. Cook for an additional 1-2 minutes, until spinach starts to wilt.
5. Add egg mixture and cook for 4 minutes, not stirring. Top with bacon pieces and cook an additional 1-2 minutes until the eggs just begin to set.
6. Put pan in the preheated oven and bake for 8 to 12 minutes.

Easy Egg and Salsa

Serves: 1
Preparation time: 5 minutes
Cooking time: 10 minutes

Ingredients:
- 2 eggs
- 1 avocado
- 1-2 Tbsp. salsa

Instructions:
1. Soft boil two eggs by bringing water in a pot to a boil, then adding eggs. Boil for 5 minutes.
2. In the meantime, dice the avocado and put on a plate.
3. Top with soft boiled eggs, cut up. Add salsa and serve.

Cream Cheese Pancakes

Serves: 4 pancakes
Preparation time: 8 minutes
Cooking time: 15 minutes

Ingredients:

- 2 oz. full-fat cream cheese, softened
- 2 eggs
- 1 tsp. Stevia
- ¼ tsp. cinnamon
- ¼ tsp. nutmeg
- 1 Tbsp. olive oil

Instructions:

1. Combine all ingredients except olive oil in a blender. Blend until smooth and let it sit for about 2 minutes.
2. Heat olive oil in a pan over medium heat. Pour ¼ of batter in the hot pan. Cook for 2 minutes, until bubble start to appear on the top. Flip and cook for an additional minute. Repeat with the rest of the batter, and serve with fresh berries.

Baked Spiced Granola

Serves: 4
Preparation time: 5 minutes
Cooking time: 2 minutes

Ingredients:
- 1 ¼ cup pecans, chopped
- 1/3 cup walnuts, chopped
- 2/3 cup almonds, slivered
- ¾ cup coconut
- 2/3 cup almond meal
- 2/3 cup flax meal
- 1/3 cup pumpkin seeds
- 1/3 cup sunflower seeds
- 1/3 cup butter, melted
- 2/3 cup sweetener
- 1 tsp. pure honey
- ½ tsp. cinnamon
- 1 tsp. vanilla extract
- ¼ tsp. nutmeg
- Pinch salt
- ¼ - 1/3 cup water

Instructions:
1. Heat oven to 250 degrees (F).
2. In bowl, combine all ingredients, mixing well.
3. Line a cookie sheet with parchment paper and spray with cooking spray.
4. Spread the mixture on the tray. Add a second piece of parchment paper on top and roll over the granola with a rolling pin to press it into a firm sheet. Discard top sheet of parchment paper.
5. Bake for an hour to 90 minutes, checking and stirring every 15 minutes. When baked to desired consistency, remove and let it cool before serving.
6. This can be kept in a sealed container until needed.

Eggs Benedict

Serves: 2
Preparation time: 10 minutes
Cooking time: 20 minutes

Ingredients:

- 4 strips bacon, raw
- 4 eggs
- 1 stick butter
- 3 egg yolks
- 3 Tbsp. lemon juice
- Pinch cayenne
- 1 Tbsp. water

Instructions:

1. Heat oven to 375 degrees (F).
2. Line four muffin cups with a strip of raw bacon, and break egg into bacon cup.
3. Bake for 15 to 20 minutes.
4. Meanwhile, make the sauce. Melt the butter in a microwave-safe bowl in the microwave. In a second bowl, mix egg yolks, lemon juice, cayenne and water. Add melted butter to the egg mixture, 1 tablespoon at a time. Combine thoroughly. Microwave for 30 seconds, stirring every 10 seconds.
5. When eggs are cooked, remove from heat and top with sauce. Enjoy!

Turkey and Zucchini Breakfast Quiche

Serves: 10
Preparation time: 20 minutes
Cooking time: 45 minutes

Ingredients:

For the Crust

- 2 cup almond flour
- Pinch of salt
- 1 Tbsp. + 1 tsp. coconut oil (divided)
- 1 egg, large
- 1 tsp. water

For the Filling

- 1 cup ground turkey
- ¼ cup onion
- 6 eggs, large
- 2/3 cup half and half
- 1 tsp, fennel seed
- 1 tsp. oregano
- Salt and pepper to taste
- 1 ½ cup zucchini, grated

Instructions:

1. Heat oven to 350 degrees (F).
2. Assemble crust by pulsing almond flour and salt in a food processor. Add coconut oil, egg, and water. Pulse until the dough forms a ball.
3. Lightly grease pie pan and press ball into the bottom and sides of the pan. Set aside.
4. Next, brown the ground turkey and onion in large pan. Cool for a few minutes.
5. Whisk eggs in a bowl until smooth. Add half and half and spices. Mix thoroughly.
6. Add zucchini and turkey to the egg mixture, and mix together.
7. Add filling to pie crust. Bake in oven for about 35 to 40 minutes, until the center is firm.
8. If desired, top servings with 1 Tbsp. sour cream and serve.

Keto Porridge

Serves: 2
Preparation time: 5 minutes
Cooking time: 5 minutes

Ingredients:

- 2 Tbsp. chia seeds
- 3 Tbsp. sesame seeds
- 2 eggs
- ¾ cup heavy cream
- Salt and pepper to taste
- 5 ⅓ Tbsp. heavy whipping cream
- 1 pinch salt
- 2 tsp. coconut oil

Instructions:

1. Combine all ingredients except the oil. Set aside.
2. Next, heat oil in small pan, and add mixture. Stir until porridge reaches a firm consistency. Simmer but do not boil.
3. Serve with berries.

Low Carb Cajun Cauli Hash

Serves: 2
Preparation time: 10 minutes
Cooking time: 15 minutes

Ingredients:

- 2 Tbsp. olive oil
- 2/3 cup onion, diced
- 2 Tbsp. garlic, minced
- 2 cup cauliflower, steamed and chopped evenly
- 1-2 tsp. Cajun seasoning
- 1 cup pastrami, shaved and chopped to 1 inch pieces
- ½ - ¾ green pepper, raw and diced to ¼ inch pieces

Instructions:

1. Sauté onions in olive oil over medium heat for about 5 minutes.
2. Add garlic and sauté for additional 2 minutes.
3. Squeeze any liquid from the cauliflower. Add to mixture and sauté for 5-10 minutes or until crispy and brown.
4. Add Cajun seasoning, pastrami and pepper. Cook, stirring frequently, for about 5 minutes.
5. If desired, cook two eggs.
6. Place cooked hash in bowls, top with optional eggs and serve.

Keto Bread

This bread could be lightly toasted as a perfect accompaniment for a traditional eggs and bacon meal.

Serves: 2 loafs
Preparation time: 10 minutes
Cooking time: 30 minutes

Ingredients:
- 12 eggs, yolks and whites separated
- ½ tsp. cream of tartar
- 3 cup almond flour
- 1 stick butter, melted
- 1 ½ tsp. baking soda
- 2 Tbsp. apple cider vinegar

Instructions:
1. Heat oven to 350 degrees (F).
2. Combine egg whites. Add cream of tartar and using mixer, whip until there are soft peaks.
3. Combine remaining ingredients to a food processor. Pulse until combined well.
4. Place batter in a bowl and fold in egg white mixture gently.
5. Grease two loaf pans, and add ½ of mixture to each pan.
6. Bake for 30-35 minutes or until brown. Let it cool before cutting.

Appetizers & Snacks

Bacon Poblano Hot Crab Dip

Serves: 8-10
Preparation time: About 10 minutes
Cooking time: 20-22 minutes

Ingredients:

- 8 strips bacon
- ½ cup cream cheese, softened
- 1/3 cup mayonnaise
- 2/3 cup sour cream
- 4-5 green onion, diced
- 2 peppers, diced
- 4-5 garlic cloves, minced
- 3 Tbsp. lemon juice
- 1 cup Parmesan cheese, separated
- 1 ½ cup crab meat (not imitation)

Instructions:

1. Heat oven to 350 degrees (F).
2. Cook bacon in a pan over medium high heat until crispy. Drain and let the bacon cool on a paper towel to absorb excess grease.
3. Combine cream cheese, mayonnaise and sour cream and mix with a mixer. Don't worry about removing all the lumps; a little clumpy is fine for this recipe.
4. Next, add in the green onion, pepper, cooked bacon, garlic, lemon juice, and ½ cup of Parmesan cheese. Mix on a low setting until everything is well combined.
5. With a rubber spatula, gently fold in the crab meat. Be careful not to break the crab meat up to much; chunks are a great component of this dish.
6. Pour into pie pan or similar oven safe dish. Spread into an even layer. Finally top with other ½ cup of Parmesan cheese.
7. Bake for 20-22 minutes. If desired, finish under low broiler for 1 to 2 minutes until the top is golden brown.
8. Serve warm.
9. This dip can be served with carrot sticks, celery sticks, cucumber slices or even pork rinds.

White Chocolate Fat Bomb

Serves: 16
Preparation time: 5 minutes
Cooking time: 10 minutes

Ingredients:

- ½ cup cocoa butter
- ½ cup coconut oil
- 15-20 drops vanilla flavored Stevia

Instructions:

1. In a double boiler, melt cocoa butter and coconut oil. When well combined, remove from heat and add vanilla Stevia drops. Stir thoroughly and pour into desired molds, such as silicone baking cups.
2. Chill for 15 minutes, or until completely hardened.
3. Remove bombs from the molds and keep refrigerated in tightly sealed storage container.

Creamy Coconut Ice Cream

Serves: 4
Preparation time: 10 minutes + Freezing time

Ingredients:

- 4 eggs, pasteurized
- 4 egg yolks, pasteurized
- 1 Tbsp. vanilla
- ½ tsp. apple cider vinegar
- 1 stick butter
- 6 Tbsp. coconut oil
- 3 Tbsp. + 2 tsp. XCT oil
- 5 Tbsp. erythritol
- About ½ cup ice

Instructions:

1. In a blender, combine all the ingredients except the ice. This is going to take some time to get the butter blended to a nice, creamy consistency.
2. Once it becomes creamy, add in the ice and blend until well combined and the consistency of yogurt for a creamy end result. If you prefer a firmer ice cream, add 1 or 2 more ice cubes when blending.
3. Pour the mixture into an ice cream maker and follow your manufacturer's instructions until ice cream is ready.

Kale Chips

Serves: 4
Preparation time: 5 minutes
Cooking time: 15 minutes

Instructions:

- 2 bunches of kale
- 4 Tbsp. coconut oil
- 4 Tbsp. Parmesan cheese
- 1 Tbsp. garlic salt
- 2 tsp. crushed red pepper, optional

Instructions:

1. Heat oven to 350 degrees (F).
2. Thoroughly wash and dry kale bunches. (Make sure the kale is thoroughly dried with paper towels, otherwise it will steam instead of bake, and may burn before getting crispy.)
3. Remove tough stems and rip kale into consistent desired pieces.
4. Mix the rest of the ingredients and gently rub the oil and seasonings into the kale, making sure to coat both sides of each leaf.
5. When the leaves are shiny with oil, lay them out on two cookie sheets lined with parchment paper.
6. Bake kale for about 15-20 minutes, gently turning them over after about 7 to 10 minutes.
7. When crunchy, take them out and let the kale chips cool before storing. Store in an airtight bowl until ready to snack.

Tuna Salad

Serves: 2
Preparation time: 15 minutes

Ingredients:
- 2 eggs
- 4 slices bacon
- 2 cans light tuna
- ¼ onion
- 3 Tbsp. mayonnaise

Instructions:
1. Make hard boil eggs.
2. Meanwhile, cook bacon to until crispy. Remove from heat and place bacon on a paper towel.
3. Chop onion and hard boiled eggs separately.
4. Drain tuna and put in a bowl.
5. Add both the chopped egg and onion. Crumble bacon and add with mayo. Combine thoroughly.
6. This is great for lunch or a snack. Half a cucumber, scoop out the seeds and add the tuna salad. Enjoy!

Crispy Cheddar Cheese Chips

Serves: 6
Preparation time: 5 minutes
Cooking time: 20-25 minutes

Ingredients:

- 6 cup cheddar cheese, shredded
- ¾ tsp. onion powder
- ½ tsp. garlic powder
- ½ tsp. paprika
- ¼ tsp. chili powder
- ¼ tsp. cumin
- Pinch sea salt

Instructions:

1. Heat oven to 400 degrees (F).
2. Line two medium baking sheets with parchment paper. Overlap the sides with parchment, so the chips will be easy to take out after baked.
3. Thoroughly mix all ingredients together in a large bowl.
4. Divide mixture in half and spread them into the baking sheets, forming a rectangle. The straighter the edges, the better to make a consistent sized chip.
5. Bake mixture for 18-20 minutes, or until the chips are noticeably crisp.
6. Remove from oven, and lift the cheese off the sheets, using the overlapped sides of the parchment paper. If the cheese seems to be too pliable, put it back in the oven and cook for 1-2 more minutes.
7. Place the cheese sheets on a smooth, cool countertop or cutting board.
8. Let cool for 2 minutes.
9. Take a pizza cutter and slice the cheese into triangles. Store in an airtight container in the fridge until ready to eat.

Granola Bars

Serves: 14
Preparation time: 10 minutes
Cooking time: 20 minutes

Ingredients:

- 3 cup assorted nuts and seeds, such as almonds or walnut pumpkin, sesame or sunflower seeds.
- 2/3 cup coconut, unsweetened
- 2 eggs, large
- 3 Tbsp. cocoa nibs
- 1/3 cup coconut oil
- 4 Tbsp. almond butter
- 1 ½ tsp. vanilla extract
- 1 tsp. cinnamon
- Pinch sea salt
- 3 Tbsp. Stevia

Instructions:

1. Heat oven to 350 degrees. (F)
2. Combine all ingredients in a blender. Pulse until the mixture is combined. Do not overmix, because there should still be visible pieces of seeds and nuts.
3. Grease ovenproof 8x10 casserole dish. Place mixture in the dish and press lightly to ensure a consistent layer.
4. Bake for 18-20 minutes, until bars are brown. Don't overcook.
5. Remove dish and allow it to cool for 10 minutes.
6. Turn upside down onto a cutting board or baking sheet and carefully cut into 14 'bars'. These can be drizzled with melted chocolate or dusted with unsweetened coconut, if desired.
7. Store in an airtight container.

Kale Pate

Serves: 10
Preparation time: 10 minutes
Cooking time: 5 minutes

Ingredients:
- 1 bunch kale
- 2/3 cup + 1 Tbsp. olive oil, separated
- 2/3 cup sesame seeds
- 7-8 green onions
- 3 Tbsp. apple cider vinegar
- Salt and pepper, to taste

Instructions:
1. Wash and thoroughly dry kale. Chop it into small pieces.
2. Combine kale with the 1 Tbsp. olive oil. Cook it in a cast iron pan, covered, for about 7-8 minutes over a low heat, stirring occasionally.
3. Remove toasted kale and put in a blender or food processor with the remaining ingredients.
4. Blend until the mixture is smooth, stirring as needed.
5. Store in an airtight container. Pate can be kept for 4-5 days in the refrigerator.
6. Kale pate can be served with zucchini, carrot, or celery sticks or cucumber slices.

Greek Stuffed Mushrooms

Serves: 12
Preparation time: 15 minutes
Cooking time: 10 minutes

Ingredients:
- 1/8 cup olive oil
- 3 cloves garlic, minced
- ¾ lb. ground lamb
- ¼ cup onion, diced
- 3-5 fresh basil leaves + extra for topping
- Sea salt and fresh pepper, to taste
- 12 baby portabella mushrooms

Toppings:
- ½ cup feta cheese
- 6 sun dried tomatoes

Instructions:
1. Heat oven to 350 (F).
2. Heat oil in a cast iron frying pan and sauté garlic for 1 minute.
3. Add ground lamb and onion and brown thoroughly. Remove from heat.
4. Meanwhile, soak sundried tomatoes. When rehydrated, cut in half. Set aside.
5. Gently tear basil leaves and stir into lamb mixture, along with salt and pepper.
6. Wash mushrooms and remove stems. Place mushroom caps upside down on a cookie sheet lined with parchment.
7. In the mushroom cap, add ½ sun dried tomato, then the lamb mixture. Top with whole basil leaf, then 1 tsp. feta.
8. Put mushrooms in the oven and bake for 8-10 minutes.

Curried Zucchini Crisps

Serves: 4
Preparation time: 15 minutes
Cooking time: 60 minutes

Ingredients:

- 3 zucchini, medium.
- 4 tsp. olive oil
- ¼ tsp. curry powder
- ¼ tsp. garlic salt

Instructions:

1. Heat oven to 225 degrees (F).
2. Line two baking sheets with a double layer of parchment paper.
3. Cut and discard zucchini ends. With a mandolin, slice zucchini into very thin slices. If you don't have a mandolin, take a sharp knife and carefully slice zucchini as thin as possible.
4. Place zucchini slices on the baking sheets in a single layer. They can be placed close together, but make sure they don't touch.
5. Combine the curry powder and garlic salt in a bowl.
6. Brush zucchini with olive oil, then sprinkle spice mixture over the top.
7. Bake for 45 minutes to 1 hour. After ½ hour, check every 10 minutes to make sure they are becoming crisp but not burned.
8. When crisp, remove from oven. In the event that some are done sooner than others, they might need to be removed before the full batch so they don't burn.
9. Let the zucchini chips cool on the cookie sheet. When cool, remove with a spatula and keep fresh in an airtight container.

Fruit & Veggie Smoothie Leathers

Serves: 5
Preparation time: 10 minutes
Cooking time: 6 hours

Instructions:

- 6-8 carrots, juiced
- 3-4 utility apples, juiced
- 1 banana, ripe
- 1 mango
- 1 cup strawberries
- 1/3 cup chia seeds
- ¾ cup carrot and apple pulp

Instructions:

1. Combine all ingredients. Add to a blender and blend until smooth. The mixture can either be dehydrated or baked in the oven.
2. If using a dehydrator, spread the mixture on fruit leather sheet that came with the food dehydrator. The mixture should be about 1/8 of an inch thick. Dehydrate at 105 degree setting for 5-6 hours.
3. If using the oven, heat oven to 150 degrees (F), or the lowest possible oven setting. Line a baking sheet with parchment paper. If using small baking sheets, you may need to divide the mixture between 2 sheets, to get it to the 1/8-inch thickness. Place sheet or sheets in the oven and bake for 6-8 hours until the mixture is set and not tacky to the touch. Depending on your oven's temperature, start checking the mixture at 6 hours and check every 20 minutes to a half hour until done. When done, remove from the oven and let cool thoroughly.
4. When cooled, use a pizza cutter to cut the leather into either squares or strips. These can be turned into a fruity roll up by rolling the strips in parchment paper. If keeping in strips or squares, separate layers with parchment paper. Keep fresh in an airtight container.

Cheddar-Wrapped Taco Rolls

Serves: 3
Preparation time: 15 minutes
Cooking time: 25-30 minutes

Ingredients:

- 2 cup Mexican cheese blend
- 1 cup ground turkey
- Taco seasoning
- 1 tomato, chopped
- ½ cup avocado, chopped
- 1 Tbsp. taco sauce
- Other taco toppings, as desired

Instructions:

1. Heat oven to 400 degrees (F).
2. Line a baking sheet with parchment paper. Overlap the sides with parchment, so the baked cheese will be easy to take out after it is ready.
3. Sprinkle shredded cheese mix over the baking sheet, enough to cover it with one layer.
4. Put sheet in the oven and bake for 12-15 minutes until the cheese begins to bubble and turns a toasty brown.
5. After removing from the oven, test doneness by sliding a spatula under the edges to make sure it is a solid piece. If not, return it to the oven and bake for a few more minutes, until it passes the spatula test.
6. When ready, add the taco meat in a layer over the cheese layer and cook for 8-10 more minutes.
7. While that is cooking, combine the other toppings. When preparing the toppings, make sure the pieces are small enough that they will easily become a thin layer on top of the meat mixture.
8. When the taco layer is cooked, take it out of the oven.
9. Holding the sides of the parchment paper, take out the hot layer, keeping it on the parchment.
10. Add the taco toppings in a single, thin layer on top of the meat layer.
11. Slice into 3 or 4 even slices.
12. Roll the slices and serve. You can add a spooful of sour cream, if desired.

Keto Oatmeal Chocolate Chip Cookies

Serves: 18
Preparation time: 10 minutes
Cooking time: 18 minutes

Ingredients:
- 1 ¼ cup almond flower
- 1/3 cup sunflower seeds, ground
- 1/3 cup coconut
- 2 Tbsp. all-spice
- ¼ cup fermented vegan proteins+, unflavored/unsweetened (found in health food stores or online)
- ¾ tsp. baking powder
- Pinch sea salt
- ½ cup coconut oil
- 1/3 cup granulated Stevia
- 1 egg
- 1 tsp. vanilla
- 2/3 cup Stevia-sweetened chocolate chips

Instructions:
1. Heat oven to 325 degrees (F).
2. Line two baking sheets with parchment paper. You can also use silicone baking sheets instead of parchment paper.
3. Combine almond flour, ground sunflower seeds, coconut, allspice, vegan proteins, baking powder and salt in a bowl. Mix well.
4. Next, combine the coconut oil, stevia, egg and vanilla in a mixing bowl. Mix on a low setting for 30 seconds, then for 1 minute on a medium setting until creamy.
5. Add dry ingredients and mix for another 15 to 30 seconds. Be careful to combine but not overmix.
6. Carefully fold in chocolate chips until fully mixed with the dough.
7. Roll about a tablespoon of dough into your hands. If the dough sticks, use a bit of coconut oil to coat your hands. Place ball on a cookie sheet, and press down carefully.
8. Repeat the process until you have made 18 cookies, keeping them an inch apart from each other and the sides.
9. Place baking sheets in the oven and bake for 16 to 18 minutes. When they are done, they'll be a light golden brown and the sides will be a little cracked.
10. Remove baking sheets from the oven and allow it to cool for 2 minutes. Using a spatula, transfer to a cooling rack. Ideally, cool for another 10 minutes, then enjoy, either alone or with a glass of almond or coconut milk.
11. If there are any leftovers, store in an air tight container.

Keto Vanilla Shortbread Cookies

Serves: 16
Preparation time: 15 minutes
Cooking time: 20-25 minutes

Ingredients:

- 2 ¼ cup almond flour
- 1/3 cup Stevia or equivalent
- Pinch sea salt
- 1 tsp. vanilla extract
- 1 stick butter, softened
- 1 egg

Instructions:

1. Heat oven to 300 degrees (F).
2. Combine the flour, Stevia, salt and vanilla extract.
3. Next, add the butter and mix with the dry ingredients.
4. Finally, add the egg and mix well to form a dough.
5. Roll about a tablespoon of dough into your hands. If the dough sticks, use a bit of coconut oil to coat your hands.
6. Place ball on a cookie sheet, and press down carefully. Repeat the process until you have made 18 cookies, keeping them an inch apart from each other and the sides.
7. Bake cookies for 20 to 25 minutes, or until the edges are lightly browned. The cookies will be soft when you take them from the oven, but will become firmer as they cool down.
8. Remove baking sheets from the oven and allow it to cool for 2 minutes. Using a spatula, transfer to a cooling rack. Ideally, cool for another 10 minutes, then enjoy, either alone or with a glass of almond or coconut milk.
9. If there are any leftovers, store in an air tight container.

Roasted Spiced Vanilla Cashews

Serves: 4
Preparation time: 5 minutes + overnight
Cooking time: 3 hours

Ingredients:
- 2/3 cup vanilla extract
- 2/3 cup water
- 1 ¼ cup nuts (ideally cashews, almonds or a combination of the two)
- 3 Tbsp. cinnamon or all-spice

Instructions:
1. Combine vanilla and water in a bowl.
2. Add the nuts, and cover. Allow them to soak overnight.
3. After 8 hours or overnight, spread the nuts on a layer of paper towels and allow them to completely dry. This will likely take a few hours, depending on the air temperature and moisture content.
4. Next, heat the oven to 200 degrees (F).
5. Line a cookie sheet with parchment paper. Add nuts and spread out evenly.
6. Sprinkle with the cinnamon or allspice.
7. Bake the nuts in the oven for about 3 hours, making sure to stir every 30 minutes to prevent the nuts from burning.
8. When ready, remove from oven and allow it to cool completely. Store in an airtight container.

Macadamia Nut Hummus

Serves: 8-10
Preparation time: 5 minutes

Ingredients:

- 2/3 cup macadamia nuts, roasted
- 1 (16 oz.) can of garbanzo beans, drained
- 2 Tbsp. olive oil or coconut oil
- 4 tsp. lemon juice
- 2-3 Tbsp. water
- 2 cloves garlic, minced
- Handful (8-10) basil leaves
- Salt and pepper, as desired

Instructions:

1. Combine all ingredients in a food processor blender.
2. Puree until achieving a smooth consistency. If it is too lumpy, add 1 tsp. water and blend again.
3. Store in an airtight container. This is delicious served with zucchini, carrot, or celery sticks or cucumber slices.

Mini Pumpkin Spice Muffins

Serves: 20 mini muffins
Preparation time: 10 minutes
Cooking time: 14-16 minutes

Ingredients:
- 8 oz. canned pumpkin
- 1/3 cup Sunbutter or equivalent
- 1 egg
- 1/3 cup erythritol or stevia
- 1/3 cup organic coconut flour, sifted
- 2 Tbsp. flaxseed meal
- 1 tsp. all-spice
- ½ tsp. baking soda
- ½ tsp. baking powder
- Pinch of salt
- 1 Tbsp. cream cheese

Instructions:
1. Heat oven to 350 degrees (F).
2. Coat mini muffin pan with cooking spray.
3. In a mixing bowl, blend pumpkin, Sunbutter and egg until smooth.
4. Add remaining ingredients. Mix thoroughly.
5. Scoop about 1 tablespoon of batter into each prepared baking cups.
6. Bake for 14-16 minutes. Remove from oven and allow it to cool in baking cups.
7. Remove from the cups and serve.
8. These can be stored for three days in an airtight container. They can also be refrigerated for a week, or frozen for up to a month. If refrigerated or frozen, allow it to come up to room temperature before serving.

Cheesy Cauliflower Muffins

Serves: 12 muffins
Preparation time: 15 minutes
Cooking time: 20-25 minutes

Ingredients:

- 3 cup cauliflower 'rice' (see "Cauliflower Fritters" recipe for instructions on how to rice cauliflower)
- 2 eggs
- 1 cup cheddar cheese, shredded, separated into ½ cup measurements
- ¼ cup almond flour
- ½ tsp. baking powder
- 2/3 tsp. dry Italian seasoning herb blend
- ¼ to 1/3 tsp. onion powder
- ¼ tsp. garlic powder

Instructions:

1. Heat oven to 375 degrees (F).
2. Prepare muffin tin with cooking spray or Line muffin pan with cupcake liners. If possible, use parchment liners, because the muffins will not stick.
3. Mix cauliflower 'rice' with eggs, the ½ cup cheese, almond flour, baking powder and seasonings. Stir until smooth.
4. Fill prepared muffin tins. Sprinkle the other ½ cup of cheese on the top.
5. Bake for 20-25 minutes. To test for doneness, lightly press on the top of the muffin with your finger to ensure it isn't wet to the touch and springs back easily.

Bacon Jalapeno Poppers

Serves: 18 poppers
Preparation time: 5 minutes
Cooking time: 40 minutes

Ingredients:
- ½ lb. ground beef or ground turkey
- ¼ tsp. onion powder
- Salt and pepper, to taste
- 9 medium jalapeno peppers
- 2 -3 oz. cream cheese, softened
- 8 slices bacon

Instructions:
1. Heat oven to 400 degrees (F).
2. Put ground meat in a cast iron frying pan with onion powder, salt and pepper. Cook on medium heat until completely browned. Set aside to allow it to cool.
3. Next, cut jalapeno peppers horizontally in half. Remove the seeds.
4. Put a thin layer of cream cheese in the bottom of each pepper half, but be careful not to put too much cream cheese in.
5. Add ground beef mixture.
6. Slice each piece of bacon in half, the long way.
7. Wrap the bacon half around the pepper, making sure you 'trap' all the filling in with the bacon.
8. Put prepared jalapenos on a lined cookie sheet. For better results, put a baking rack on the lined sheet and snug the peppers in between the tines. Bake for 30 minutes.

Fish & Poultry

Pan Seared Salmon with Lemon Dill Sauce

Serves: 4
Preparation time: 15 minutes
Cooking time: 15 minutes

Ingredients:

- 4 salmon fillets, 4 oz. each
- 1 tsp. garlic salt
- 2 tsp. salt
- Pepper, to taste
- 1 tsp. onion powder
- ½ stick butter
- 3 Tbsp. coconut oil
- 1/3 cup Greek yogurt
- 2/3 cup sour cream
- 2 Tbsp. olive oil
- 2 tsp. fresh dill or 1 Tbsp. dried dill
- 4 Tbsp. lemon juice
- 1 tsp. Tabasco sauce

Instructions:

1. In a bowl, combine garlic salt, pepper and onion powder. Sprinkle over the salmon and then lightly rub it into the meat. Reserve whatever seasoning you didn't use.
2. Next, heat coconut oil in a cast iron frying pan for about 2 minutes over medium high heat.
3. Sear the filets, face down, for about 2-3 minutes until you can see it cooked halfway up the filet. Carefully flip the fish and sear the other side for 3 minutes.
4. Remove from heat, but keep the fish in the pan for another 1-2 minutes to make sure the fish is completely cooked. Test for doneness by flaking the fish with a fork. If it doesn't flake, it is not done.
5. When the salmon is cooked, top each filet with about 1 tablespoon of butter allowing it to melt down the fish.
6. Mix the unused spice mixture with the remaining ingredients. Top the salmon with the sauce and serve.

Fish Cakes with Aioli

Serves: 6
Preparation time: 30 minutes
Cooking time: 10 minutes

Ingredients:

- 2 cup cauliflower rice (see "Cauliflower Fritters" recipe for instructions on how to rice cauliflower)
- ¼ cup ghee, separated
- 4 cloves garlic, minced and separated
- 2 lb. white haddock or other white fish
- Salt and pepper to taste
- 1 tsp. lemon zest
- 1 tsp. cumin
- 2 Tbsp. freshly chopped parsley or 3 Tbsp. dried parsley
- 2 eggs
- 1 yellow onion, diced
- ½ cup grated Parmesan cheese
- ¼ cup flax meal

For Aioli:

- 2/3 cup mayonnaise
- 2 cloves garlic, minced

Instructions:

1. Start by warming the cauliflower rice.
2. Then, grease a medium saucepan with 1 tablespoon of ghee with 2 cloves of minced garlic.
3. Sauté over medium heat for 30 seconds or so, or until fragrant.
4. Then, add the cauliflower rice along with a dash of salt. Cook, stirring frequently, for 5 to 7 minutes. Remove from heat and set aside.
5. Next, cook the fish. First, pat dry the filets with a paper towel and then season with a bit of salt and pepper.
6. Heat a large cast iron frying pan with ghee over medium high heat. When hot, add fish. Cook for 2 to 3 minutes, then carefully flip and cook the other side.
7. When ready, the fish will flake when tested with a fork.
8. Transfer cooked fish to a bowl and set aside, allowing it to cool for 8 to 10 minutes.

9. In a bowl, combine rice mixture with lemon zest, cumin, parley, eggs, onion, Parmesan cheese and flax meal, along with remaining salt and pepper, stirring until combined well. Fold in cool fish.
10. Assemble the patties, using a quarter cup measuring cup to estimate the amount. You can either use a cutting board to assemble the patties, or use your hands to form the 18 patties.
11. Cook the patties, 3 at a time in a large frying pan with a tablespoon of ghee over medium high heat. Cook 3-5 minutes on one side, until golden. Don't flip until they are ready or you might crack the crust and crumble the resulting patty.
12. Keep cooked patties warm in the oven until ready.
13. Prepare aioli by combing mayonnaise and minced garlic. Add a dash of salt and pepper as desired. Serve with aioli either on top of the patties or on to the side.

White Fish In Herbed Butter

Serves: 4
Preparation time: 5 minutes
Cooking time: 15 minutes

Ingredients:

- ½ cup butter, softened
- 1 tsp. fresh dill, or 2 tsp. dried dill
- ½ tsp. onion powder
- 1 tsp. garlic salt
- Pepper to taste
- 2 to 2 ½ lbs. haddock or other white fish

Instructions:

1. In a small bowl, mix all the ingredients but the fish. Set aside to let it blend.
2. Next, heat a cast iron frying pan over medium heat. Add butter mixture and allow it to heat for 1 minute.
3. Add fish. Sauté one side for 6 to 7 minutes, then flip and cook and additional 6 to 7 minutes.
4. Serve with lemon wedges.

Shrimp Chow Mein

Serves: 2-3
Preparation time: 15 minutes
Cooking time: 55-60 minutes

Ingredients:
- 1 medium spaghetti squash
- 3 garlic cloves, minced
- 1/3 tsp. ginger, minced
- 3 green onions, diced.
- 2 chili peppers, diced
- 8-10 peppercorns
- 1 Tbsp. sesame oil
- 1 lb. shrimp, peeled and deveined
- 4 cup coleslaw mix
- ¼ cup coconut aminos
- Salt, to taste
- Pinch of coconut sugar (optional)

Instructions:
1. Heat oven to 375 degrees (F).
2. Slice the squash in half, lengthwise. Bake for 45-50 minutes or until tender.
3. When done, remove from heat. Use a fork to remove the insides and shred it into 'spaghetti'.
4. Next, mix the garlic, ginger, onion, peppers and peppercorns.
5. Heat sesame oil in a cast iron frying pan over medium heat. Stir fry the garlic mixture for about 30 seconds or until fragrant.
6. Add shrimp. Cook until the shrimp is pink on both sides, stirring often so the mixture doesn't burn.
7. Add the coleslaw mix. Cook for another 1 to 2 minutes or until the coleslaw mix is softened slightly.
8. Finally, add the spaghetti squash. Stir the mixture until well combined.
9. Add the coconut aminos and toss together. Salt as necessary, and, if desired, add coconut sugar to bring out the sweetness of the shrimp.

Easy Keto Shrimp Scampi

Serves: 6
Preparation time: 15 minutes
Cooking time: 60 minutes

Ingredients:

- 1 medium spaghetti squash
- 1 Tbsp. olive oil
- 3 Tbsp. butter
- 1 clove of garlic, minced
- 2/3 cup dry white wine
- Salt and pepper, to taste
- Pinch of red pepper flakes, optional
- 2 ½ lbs. extra large shrimp, cooked, peeled and deveined
- Juice of 1 lemon
- 1 tsp. lemon zest
- ¼ cup fresh parsley, chopped

Instructions:

1. Heat oven to 375 degrees (F).
2. Slice the squash in half, lengthwise. Bake for 45-50 minutes or until tender. When done, remove from heat. Use a fork to remove the insides and shred it into 'spaghetti'.
3. Next, combine oil and butter in a large saucepan.
4. Add the garlic. Sauté for 2 or 3 minutes, until fragrant.
5. Add wine and seasonings. Cook for an additional 2 minutes.
6. Add shrimp and heat for 1 to 2 minutes.
7. Remove from heat. Stir in lemon juice and zest, as well as parsley.
8. Serve with hot spaghetti squash. If desired, top with grated Parmesan cheese.

Creamy Keto Fish Casserole

Serves: 5
Preparation time: 10 minutes
Cooking time: 30 minutes

Ingredients:

- 1 ½ lbs. broccoli
- 3 Tbsp. olive oil
- 6 scallions, chopped
- 3 Tbsp. capers
- 2 lbs. white fish, cut into 5 serving sized pieces
- 1 ½ cup heavy cream
- 1 Tbsp. Dijon mustard
- 1 Tbsp. parsley
- Salt and pepper, to taste
- 5 Tbsp. butter

For serving:

- 1 cup leafy greens

Instructions:

1. Heat oven to 400 degrees (F).
2. First, cut broccoli into florets. Include the stem, but peel with a knife where the skin is rough.
3. Fry broccoli in a greased skilled for 5 minutes, or until al dente. Add salt and pepper as desired.
4. Next, add chopped scallions and capers. Sauté for an additional 2 minutes. Remove from heat.
5. In a greased baking dish, add the vegetables and fish portions.
6. Combine cream and mustard with the parsley and seasoning, and drizzle over fish and vegetable mix. Top fish with pats of butter.
7. Bake for 20 minutes, until the fish flakes easily with a fork.
8. Serve alone or with leafy greens.

Salmon Patties with Fresh Herbs

Serves: 5
Preparation time: 10 minutes
Cooking time: 30 minutes

Ingredients:

- 2 cans pink salmon, (14.75-oz)
- 2 Tbsp. fresh chives, chopped
- ¼ cup fresh dill, chopped
- ¼ cup Parmesan cheese, grated
- 4 oz. pork rinds, crushed
- 2 large eggs
- 1 tsp. lemon zest
- Salt and pepper, to taste
- ½ cup almond flour
- 2 Tbsp. olive oil

Instructions:

1. Open and drain both cans of pink salmon and then add to a large mixing bowl.
2. Mix the chives, dill, Parmesan cheese, crushed pork rinds, 2 large eggs, lemon zest, and the salt and pepper into the salmon.
3. Form the salmon into 3 ounce balls. I usually end up with about 10.
4. Put the almond flour on a plate. Carefully flatten each salmon patty in the palm of your hand and then dip into the almond flour. They are fragile so I like to place the patty into the flour and then scoop some of the flour on top of the salmon, and then lightly tap it down with my fingers.
5. Preheat a skillet with 2 tablespoons of olive oil. Fry the patties over medium-high heat for a few minutes on each side. They should be cooked through and browned when finished.
6. Serve two patties with some of homemade tartar sauce, and veggies.

Fish Chowder

Serves: 6
Preparation time: 10 minutes
Cooking time: 30 minutes

Ingredients:

- 5 slices bacon, chopped
- 1 onion, diced
- 2 ½ cup daikon radish, chopped
- 3 cup chicken stock
- ¾ tsp. dried thyme
- Salt and pepper, to taste
- 2 cup heavy cream
- 1 ½ lbs. haddock or other white fish
- 2 Tbsp. butter

Instructions:

1. In a cast iron frying pan, cook bacon over medium heat until crisp.
2. Remove from pan and place on a plate with paper towels to absorb excess grease. Do not discard grease.
3. Next, add onion and radish to hot bacon grease. Cook about 10 minutes or until onions are tender.
4. Add chicken stock to pan. Simmer for 8 to 10 minutes. Add spices.
5. Finally, add cream and fish. Bring to a simmer and cook until fish is cooked through, about 6 minutes or so.
6. Remove from heat. Add butter and serve.

Keto Clam Chowder

Serves: 6
Preparation time: 10 minutes
Cooking time: 20 minutes

Ingredients:

- 6-7 Tbsp. ghee or butter
- ½ cup sliced onion
- 1 head cauliflower, medium sized
- 4 cans clams
- 2 ½ cup chicken broth
- 1 ½ cup water
- Salt and pepper, to taste
- 1 spring rosemary

Instructions:

1. In a stock pot, add 2 tablespoons ghee. Melt ghee, then add onions and cover. Cook 1-2 minutes, or until translucent.
2. Separate cauliflower into 4 equal quarters.
3. Take ¾ of the cauliflower to the onion mixture, setting aside the other ¼ for later.
4. Add chicken broth, water, salt and pepper and the rest of the ghee.
5. Bring mixture to a boil, then reduce to medium heat. Cover again and cook for 10 minutes more. Remove from heat.
6. Carefully put cooked cauliflower mixture until a large blender and blend. When it's completely smooth, carefully return the mixture back into the pot.
7. Take the ¼ remaining from the cauliflower and break it into florets. Stir florets into the mixture, add clams and the rosemary.
8. Heat to a simmer, and cook for 10 to 12 minutes more. Remove from heat, then remove rosemary sprig.
9. Salt and pepper to taste and serve. If desired, top with crumbled bacon.

Lemon Chicken Skillet

Serves: 4
Preparation time: 10 minutes
Cooking time: 20 minutes

Instructions:

- 2 Tbsp. olive or coconut oil
- 1 Tbsp. Italian seasoning
- Salt and pepper, to taste
- 6 boneless, skinless chicken breasts
- 1 ½ cup chicken broth
- 5 cloves garlic, minced
- 1/3 cup lemon juice
- ½ lemon, sliced (optional)
- 1 ¼ cup broccoli florets, either fresh or frozen
- 1-2 Tbsp. butter or ghee

Instructions:

1. In a cast iron frying pan, heat oil over medium heat.
2. Rub spices into both sides of the chicken breasts.
3. When skillet is hot, add chicken breasts and brown for 4-5 minutes on each side, or until golden brown.
4. Remove chicken and set to the side.
5. In the pan, add chicken broth, garlic and lemon juice, scraping to incorporate any residual chicken pieces, and stirring frequently.
6. Return chicken to the pan and add lemon slices, as desired.
7. Simmer for 5-6 minutes, turning the chicken after about 3 minutes.
8. Next, add broccoli and sauté until the vegetable is tender and the chicken is cooked through, about 5 minutes more.
9. Remove from heat. Stir in 1 to 2 Tbsp. of butter or ghee, as well as more salt and pepper to taste. If desired, add some fresh chopped basil or top with Parmesan cheese before serving.

Shredded Chicken Chili

Serves: 4
Preparation time: 5 minutes
Cooking time: 25-30 minutes

Ingredients:

- 3 chicken breasts
- 1 onion, chopped and separated
- 1 tsp. butter or ghee
- 1 ¼ cup chicken broth
- ¾ cup diced tomatoes canned, undrained
- 1 oz. tomato paste
- 1 tsp. chili powder
- 1 tsp. cumin
- 1 tsp. garlic powder
- 1 to 2 jalapeno peppers, chopped (optional)
- 1/3 cup cream cheese, softened
- Salt and pepper, to taste

Instructions:

1. Cook chicken breasts by boiling in water with ½ onion for 12-13 minutes.
2. When the meat is cooked, remove from liquid.
3. Use two forks to shred the chicken. To save time, you can also substitute 1 rotisserie chicken, removed from the bones, or if you have extra time, cook the chicken in a slow cooker for 6-8 hours in water and onion before shredding.
4. In a Dutch oven, melt butter or ghee over medium high heat.
5. Add the rest of the onion. Cook until the onion is translucent.
6. Next, add in the rest of the ingredients, except the cream cheese. Bring to a boil, stirring frequently, and reduce heat. Simmer, covered, over medium low heat for 12-14 minutes. Remove from heat.
7. Divide the cream cheese into chunks and add to the Dutch oven. Stir until the cream cheese is melted and blended, for about 3 or 4 minutes. Remove from heat.
8. Season with salt and pepper as desired.
9. If desired, add toppings, such as cheese, sour cream, or cilantro. Serve.

Chicken Cordon Blue Casserole

Serves: 7-8
Preparation time: 15 minutes
Bake time: 30-35 minutes

Ingredients:

- 8 cup cooked chicken, shredded
- ¾ cup ham, cut into small, bite sized pieces
- ¾ stick butter, melted
- 8 oz. cream cheese, softened
- 2 Tbsp. white wine, optional
- ¼ cup lemon juice
- ¼ cup Dijon mustard
- Salt and pepper, to taste
- ½ lb. Swiss cheese slices

Instructions:

1. Heat oven to 350 degrees (F).
2. Place shredded chicken in a 9x13 inch baking dish.
3. Add a layer of ham on top.
4. In a blender, mix butter, cream cheese, white wine, lemon juice and mustard. Add a dash of salt and pepper if needed.
5. Blend until smooth and thick.
6. Spread sauce evenly over the ham later.
7. Next, lay Swiss cheese on top.
8. Bake for 35 minutes. To make the cheese even more golden, place it under a low broiler for another 2 or 3 minutes, watching carefully to prevent it from burning.

Chicken Enchilada Bowl

Serves: 6
Preparation time: 10 minutes
Bake time: 30 minutes

Ingredients:

- 3 chicken breasts
- 2/3 cup red enchilada sauce
- 4 oz. green chilies, canned
- ¼ onion, diced
- Salt and pepper, to taste
- 1/3 cup water
- 1 ½ cup cauliflower rice, frozen
- Assorted toppings, such as jalapeno peppers, cheese, tomatoes, olives and or avocado

Instructions:

1. Cook chicken breasts by boiling in water for 12-13 minutes.
2. When the meat is cooked, remove from liquid. Use two forks to shred the chicken. To save time, you can also substitute 1 rotisserie chicken, removed from the bones, or if you have extra time, cook the chicken in a slow cooker for 6-8 hours in water and onion before shredding.
3. In a saucepan, add enchilada sauce, chilies, onions, and water and the chicken.
4. Simmer, covered, over medium heat for 5 minutes.
5. Reduce heat, uncovered for 10 to 15 minutes until most of the water has been absorbed.
6. Meanwhile, prepare cauliflower rice per provided instructions. Also, prepare toppings.
7. Serve chicken mixture on top of cauliflower rice. Finish off with toppings and serve.

Chicken Parmesan

Serves: 4
Preparation time: 20 minutes
Bake time: 40 minutes

Ingredients:
- 4 chicken breasts
- 2 ½ cup pork rinds, crushed
- 3 Tbsp. Italian seasoning
- ¾ cup Parmesan cheese, grated
- 1 ½ cup naturally low carb tomato sauce
- 1 cup mozzarella cheese
- 4 medium summer squash
- ½ tsp. salt
- 3 Tbsp. garlic oil
- 1 tsp. garlic powder
- 1 ¼ cup mozzarella cheese

Instructions:
1. Heat oven to 375 degrees (F).
2. Place chicken breast in a large plastic storage bag and pound until flattened and tender.
3. In another bag combine pork rinds, Italian seasoning and Parmesan cheese. Toss until combined.
4. Add prepared chicken breasts, one at a time, and shake until completely coated.
5. Place coated chicken breasts on a cookie sheet lined with parchment paper.
6. Bake for 3-4 minutes on each side.
7. Next, lightly grease baking dish. Put a small layer of tomato sauce, add chicken breast, then sprinkle with about ¼ cup of cheese on each breast.
8. Bake for 30-40 minutes.
9. Meanwhile, take zucchini and process them with a zoodler. If you don't have a zoodler, shave strips with a vegetable peeler. Salt lightly and set aside.
10. Heat skillet to medium high with oil. Add zoodles. Cook for about 2 minutes, until hot. Add the rest of the tomato sauce, garlic powder, and heat.
11. When chicken is cooked, remove from oven.
12. Place zoodles on plate, top with chicken. If desired, add more sauce and additional cheese to each breast and serve.

Crockpot Salsa and Cheese Chicken

Serves: 3
Preparation time: 5 minutes
Bake time: 2 hours 15 minutes

Ingredients:
- 3 lbs. chicken breasts, boneless, skinless
- 4 Tbsp. olive oil, divided
- 3 cup fresh salsa
- 2 cup shredded cheese, either mozzarella or a Mexican blend

Instructions:
1. Use olive oil to lightly grease crockpot with 2 Tbsp. olive oil.
2. Add whole chicken breasts and top with salsa.
3. Cover and slow cook the chicken on high for 2 hours.
4. Next, heat oven to 425 degrees (F).
5. Lightly grease medium sized baking dish.
6. Transfer chicken and cover with salsa liquid from the crockpot, making sure to add all the liquid from the crockpot.
7. Top with cheese and put in oven. Bake for 15 minutes or until sauce and cheese has bubbled.
8. If desired, you can garnish with cilantro and or sour cream before serving.

Garlic Parmesan Chicken Thighs

Serves: 6
Preparation time: 5 minutes
Bake time: 35 minutes

Ingredients:

- 8 chicken thighs, skin-on
- 1 Tbsp. basil
- 2 Tbsp. Parmesan cheese, grated
- 1 garlic clove, minced
- 2 tsp. olive oil
- Sea salt and pepper, to taste

Instructions:

1. Heat oven to 450 degrees (F).
2. Combine basil, cheese, garlic, and ½ tsp. of olive oil. Add salt and pepper to taste. Set aside.
3. Remove extra skin and fat from chicken thighs, but keeping a single layer of skin. Create a pocket between thigh meat and skin either using your hands or a blunt instrument.
4. Divide cheese mixture evenly and stuff under the skin pocket in each thigh. Set aside.
5. Heat the rest of the olive oil in a cast iron frying pan over medium high heat.
6. Place thighs in skillet, skin side down. Cook for 5 minutes.
7. Flip the chicken to the other side and cook for 8 to 10 more minutes.
8. Next, put frying pan into the preheated oven. Bake for 15 to 20 minutes, or until the chicken is done.
9. Remove from the oven and serve.

Cream of Chicken Soup with Bacon

Serves: 5
Preparation time: 30 minutes
Bake time: 20 minutes

Ingredients:
- 8 slices bacon
- 3 Tbsp. butter
- 2 cloves garlic, diced
- ½ cup mushrooms, sliced
- ½ cup white cooking wine **or** water
- 2/3 cup coconut milk or almond milk
- 2/3 cup heavy cream
- 4 cup chicken broth
- 4 celery stalks, chopped
- 5 pieces chicken thighs, boneless, cooked and chopped
- Salt and pepper, to taste
- 3 Tbsp. fresh parsley, chopped

Instructions:
1. In Dutch oven, cook bacon over medium heat until crispy. Remove bacon, drain excess oil on paper towels and set aside.
2. Next, add 1 tablespoon butter to pot and heat.
3. Add garlic and cook 2-3 minutes, until golden.
4. Add mushrooms cook an additional 3-4 minutes, or until softened.
5. Add the wine or water. Cook until the liquid is reduced to about half.
6. Next, add coconut milk, cream and chicken broth. Mix thoroughly, then add celery and chicken. Simmer until heated, about 5 minutes more.
7. Before serving, season with salt and pepper and top with parsley and bacon. Serve.

Cheesy Spinach Stuffed Chicken Breast

Serves: 5
Preparation time: 30 minutes
Bake time: 30 minutes

Ingredients:

- 2 ½ cup chopped spinach, uncooked
- ½ cup Parmesan cheese, grated
- ½ lb. (8 oz.) cream cheese, softened
- 2/3 cup mozzarella cheese, grated
- 1 clove garlic, minced
- ¼ tsp. nutmeg
- ½ tsp. sea salt
- ½ tsp. black pepper, ground
- 5 boneless, skinless chicken breasts

For the breading:

- 3 eggs
- ½ cup almond flour
- ½ cup Parmesan cheese, grated
- 1 tsp. dried parsley
- ¼ tsp. onion powder
- 1 tsp. garlic salt
- 2 Tbsp. olive oil, for frying

Instructions:

1. First, combine spinach, ½ cup of Parmesan cheese, cream cheese, mozzarella, garlic, nutmeg and salt and pepper. Combine thoroughly.
2. Trim chicken thighs, removing all fat.
3. Place thigh in a plastic storage bag and, with a meat tenderizer, pound the meat flat. Start on the edges and work your way to the middle of the thigh. When finished, it should be about twice the size from when it started. Remove chicken and repeat with remaining pieces.
4. Spoon 1/5 of the filling mixture into the middle of each chicken cutlet and roll the edges up around it.
5. Seal in an oval shape and put, seam side down, on a sheet lined with parchment paper.
6. Place in refrigerator and chill for about 15 minutes.
7. In the meantime, scramble the eggs in a bowl.

8. On a plate or a large bowl, mix together almond flour, ½ cup Parmesan cheese, parsley, onion powder and salt.
9. Heat oven to 375 degrees.
10. Dip chicken in egg, then in the breading. Set aside.
11. Heat olive oil in a cast iron skillet. Cook chicken in hot oil until all sides are a rich golden brown.
12. When browned sufficiently, transfer to a baking pan.
13. Bake chicken in the oven for 20 to 22 minutes. You can also insert a thermometer in the center and wait until it reaches 165 degrees.
14. Remove from oven. Serve plain or, if desired, serve with marina, tomato or Alfredo sauce.

Chicken Bone Broth

Serves: 4-6
Preparation time: 15 minutes
Bake time: 60 minutes

Ingredients:
- 1 chicken carcass
- 1 yellow onion
- 1 stalk celery
- 4 cloves garlic, diced
- 1 sprig each of fresh thyme, sage and rosemary

Instructions:
1. In an electric pressure cooker, add all ingredients to the inner pot. Fill with water to the 'Max Fill' level.
2. Seal and lock the device. Press the soup button, if equipped. If not, manually set the cooker 30 minutes on the highest pressure level.
3. When ready, remove chicken carcass and remaining vegetables and herbs. Do not discard.
4. Next, insert a small mesh strainer to the large part of a canning funnel. Put funnel tip in canning gar.
5. Pour broth directly into the jars and screw on lids. Or, put the broth in freezer bags and place broth in freezer.
6. Return the chicken carcass vegetables and herbs back in the pressure cooker. This time, only fill with water hallway to the 'Max Fill' level.
7. Seal and lock the device. Press the soup button, if equipped. If not, manually set the cooker 30 minutes on the highest pressure level. When done, repeat the canning or freezing process.
8. Broth can be stored in the refrigerator for up to a week, or in the freezer for as much as 6 months.

Meats

Slow-Cooker Beef & Broccoli

Serves: 5
Preparation time: 15 minutes
Bake time: 8 hours

Ingredients:
- 2 ½ lbs. flank steak
- ¾ cup liquid aminos
- 1 ½ cup beef broth
- 4 Tbsp. Stevia or other sweetener
- 1 tsp. ginger, grated
- 4 garlic cloves, minced
- ½ tsp. red pepper flakes or to taste
- Salt and pepper, to taste
- 1 head broccoli, or a 16 oz. package of frozen broccoli
- 1 bell pepper
- 2 tsp. sesame seeds (garnish)

Instructions:
1. Preheat crockpot on low setting.
2. While heating, slice the beef into 1 to 2 inch chunks.
3. Add steak to the crockpot, along with the liquid aminos, broth, Stevia, ginger, garlic, red pepper flakes and salt.
4. Cook on a low setting for 5 to 6 hours.
5. In the meantime, cut broccoli into florets, if using fresh broccoli.
6. Slice bell pepper into large squares.
7. When the steak is ready, stir thoroughly.
8. Add broccoli and pepper.
9. Cover again and cook for an additional hour, then mix together.
10. Plate the beef mixture and garnish with sesame seeds.
11. Serve alone or, if preferred, serve with riced cauliflower.

Skillet Lasagna

Serves: 5
Preparation time: 10 minutes
Bake time: 15 minutes

Ingredients:

- 1 ½ lbs. ground beef, 80% lean
- ¼ onion, diced
- 2 tsp. sea salt
- 24 oz. jar marinara sauce
- 5 slices thin roasted chicken breast
- 1 ½ cup shredded mozzarella cheese divided, about 4 ounces
- 1 tsp. fresh oregano

Instructions:

1. Brown the beef and onion in a cast iron skillet over medium high heat.
2. Season with salt, and cook for about 5 to 7 minutes or until cooked thoroughly.
3. Add marinara sauce to the skillet, and mix well.
4. Divide beef in half, pushing it to the sides of the pan.
5. Place a layer of the chicken breast in the center of the skillet.
6. Add ½ of the cheese on the top of the chicken and put the beef mixture back on top of the cheese evenly.
7. Next, top with remaining cheese and sprinkle with oregano.
8. Cover skillet and heat on low until cheese is melted, for about 5 minutes.

Keto Crispy Sesame Beef

Serves: 4-5
Preparation time: 35-40 minutes
Bake time: 15 minutes

Ingredients:

- 1 medium to large daikon radish
- 1 ½ lbs. rib eye steak, sliced to quarter inch strips
- 4 tsp. coconut flour
- ½ tsp. guar gum
- ½ red pepper, sliced thinly
- ½ jalapeno, sliced into thin rings
- 1 green onion, diced
- 2 cloves garlic, minced
- 1 tsp. ginger
- 2 tsp. sesame oil, for frying
- ¼ cup soy sauce, or liquid aminos
- 2 tsp. oyster sauce
- 2 Tbsp. rice vinegar
- 8 drops liquid Stevia
- 1 tsp. Sriracha sauce
- 2 sesame seeds, toasted
- ¾ tsp. red pepper flakes

Instructions:

1. Slice the daikon radish with a spiralizer into noodle types of strands. Once the noodles are cut, soak in cold water for about 20-25 minutes.
2. Cut steak into strips, about one quarter inch thick.
3. Place in bowl and cover with coconut flour and guar gum. Coat all the pieces with the flour and gum mixture. Set aside for 10 minutes.
4. Slice red pepper, jalapeno and green onion. Mince garlic and ginger.
5. Heat oil in a wok over medium heat. When the oil is hot, add the ginger, red pepper and garlic. Stir fry for 2 to 3 minutes.
6. Next, add the sauces, vinegar, Stevia and sriracha. Combine thoroughly. Cook for an additional 2 minutes.
7. Add sesame seeds and red pepper flakes, stirring thoroughly.
8. In the meantime, heat about 1 inch of a cooking oil of your choice in a frying pan over high heat.

9. Add beef strips, making sure not to overcrowd the pan. Fry for 3 minutes, then turn and fry for an additional 2 to 3 minutes until the coating is a dark brown.
10. When beef is cooked, remove it from the pain and strain on paper towels. If necessary, cook the rest of the beef until it is all browned.
11. Add the beef to the wok. Stir to combine and then cook for 2 to 3 more minutes.
12. Drain the radish noodles and plate. Top each portion with the beef and sauce.
13. Top with jalapeno and green onion and serve.

Philly Cheese Steak

Serves: 2
Preparation time: 5 minutes
Bake time: 10 minutes

Ingredients:
- 3 Tbsp. olive oil
- 2 lbs. shaved steak
- ¼ cup mayonnaise
- 2 Tbsp. Dijon mustard
- ½ cup mozzarella cheese
- Romaine lettuce
- Banana peppers, optional

Instructions:
1. Heat olive oil in a cast iron frying pan.
2. Add ½ of the shaved steak, ½ cup mayo and 1 Tbsp. Dijon mustard. Sauté, mixing well.
3. Add ¼ cup mozzarella cheese and sauté until the cheese is melted.
4. Remove steak mixture.
5. Repeat the process with the rest of the beef.
6. Place 3 leaves of romaine lettuce on a plate, add ½ of the steak mixture. Serve.

Slow Cooker Beef Stew

Serves: 10
Preparation time: 10-15 minutes
Bake time: 7 hours

Instructions:

- 1 ½ lbs. stew beef
- 4 tsp. coconut flour
- ½ tsp. guar gum
- 3 Tbsp. olive oil
- 2 Tbsp. butter
- 1 onion
- 3 garlic cloves, minced
- 1 cup mushrooms, sliced
- 1 Tbsp. parsley
- 2 tsp. rosemary
- 1 ½ tsp. paprika
- Salt and pepper, to taste
- 1 tsp. thyme
- 3 Tbsp. tomato paste
- 3 Tbsp. Worcestershire sauce
- 3 Tbsp. liquid aminos
- ¾ radishes, cut into cubes
- 2 celery stalk, chopped
- 1 cup green beans
- 1 can diced tomatoes
- 5 cup beef broth
- 2 bay leaves

Instructions:

1. Coat stew beef in mixture of coconut flour and guar gum. Let it sit for 5 minutes.
2. Heat olive oil and butter in a cast iron frying pan on medium high heat.
3. Add ½ of the stew beef to quickly brown the meat, searing in the juices.
4. Once browned, remove cooked beef and set aside.
5. Repeat the process with remaining stew beef.
6. Add all the meat to the crock pot.

7. In the hot frying pan, add onions, garlic, mushrooms, and spices (omitting bay leaves). Sauté for about 3 or 4 minutes.
8. Add the cooked vegetables to the meat in the crockpot and stir.
9. Next, add the rest of the ingredients and 4 cups of water.
10. Cover and cook for 10 hours on low, or on high for 6 to 7 hours.
11. Serve.

Beef Satay

Serves: 5
Preparation time: 20 minutes
Bake time: 10 minutes

Ingredients:

For Beef Satay & Marinade:
- 1 ½ lbs. flank steak or skirt steak
- 3 Tbsp. fish sauce
- 3 Tbsp. soy sauce or liquid aminios
- 3 Tbsp. coconut sugar or honey
- ¾ tsp. coriander, ground

For Thai Peanut Sauce:
- 2/3 cup peanut butter or almond butter
- 2 tsp. chili garlic sauce
- 2 Tbsp. coconut sugar or honey
- 2 tsp. Thai red curry paste
- ½ cup canned coconut milk

Instructions:
1. If using bamboo sticks, soak them in water to prepare them for the recipe.
2. To assemble the beef satay, cut horizontally across the strip of the steak, cut 1 ½ inch strips.
3. Slide the meat onto the skewers, leaving the edge of the skewer without meat so you can hold the stick while eating. Set aside.
4. Combine fish and soy sauces with the sweetener in a baking dish.
5. Add meat, making sure to fully coat the meat with the sauce.
6. Sprinkle the steak with coriander and rub the spice in well. Set aside, allowing the meat to marinade for about 20 minutes.
7. While the steak is marinating, preheat the grill.
8. Make the Thai peanut sauce by warming the peanut butter in the microwave for a few seconds.
9. Add chile garlic sauce, honey or other sweetener and the curry paste. Using a whisk, slowly pour the coconut milk in.
10. Remove beef from marinade and discard the marinade.
11. Pour 1 to 2 tablespoons of oil over the beef, ensuring that all areas are coated. Wrap foil around the skewer handles so that you can hold them when cooking.
12. Place beef satay on the grill and cook on both sides until the meat is done.
13. Serve with the beef satay still on the stick.

Beef & Coconut Soup

Serves: 2
Preparation time: 10 minutes
Bake time: 30 minutes

Ingredients:

- 4 cubes of beef stock
- 2 ¼ cup diced beef
- 1 cup coconut milk
- 2 ½ cup water
- 1 tsp. ginger
- 1 tsp. garlic minced
- 3 carrots
- 1 yellow onion
- 1 ½ cup cherry tomatoes

Instructions:

1. Combine all the ingredients, except the tomatoes, in a large pot.
2. Cover the pot and bring it to a boil, around 5 to 8 minutes.
3. Add the tomatoes, cover again and cook for an additional 25 to 30 minutes.

Pan Fried Ground Beef & Beans

Serves: 8
Preparation time: 10 minutes
Bake time: 20 minutes

Ingredients:

- 3 lbs. ground beef
- 1 large tomato
- 2 red bell peppers
- 2 yellow bell peppers
- 2 medium carrots
- 4 garlic cloves
- 2/3 cup olive oil
- 2 Tbsp. butter
- 1 16 oz. jar tomato sauce
- Sea salt and pepper, to taste
- Cayenne pepper, optional
- 1 lb. string beans

Instructions:

4. To make the pan fried beef, first wash and dice the tomato, peppers and carrots.
5. Place garlic cloves, olive oil and butter in a pan with oil.
6. Cook over medium heat until the garlic is brown.
7. Remove the garlic from the pan.
8. Add the ground beef to the pan and cook until the meat is fully brown.
9. Once browned, add diced vegetables in a pan. Let it cook for about 5 to 7 minutes.
10. Add tomato sauce, salt, pepper and cayenne pepper.
11. Set aside the beef mixture.
12. Remove ends and steam string beans until al dente, for about 10 to 15 minutes.
13. Toss with olive oil, salt and pepper.
14. Plate the ground beef with a side of green beans and serve.

Keto Cheese Shell Taco Cups

Serves: 4
Preparation time: 10 minutes
Bake time: 10 minutes

Ingredients:

Cheese cups:
- 8 slices of Colby jack cheese or other preferred cheese

Salsa:
- 3 Roma tomatoes, diced
- 1 jalapeno pepper, seeds removed and diced
- ¼ cup red onion, diced
- 3 Tbsp. lime juice
- 2 Tbsp. cilantro
- Assorted taco toppings, such as sour cream and taco meat

Instructions:

1. Heat oven to 375 degrees (F).
2. Line a baking sheet with parchment paper and lay down slices of cheese, with an inch between slices.
3. Bake cheese for 5 minutes or until bubbly. The edges will begin turning brown.
4. Remove from oven and let cool for a minute or two.
5. Using a spatula, carefully slide up a slice of cheese onto the utensil.
6. Transfer the cheese into a muffin tin to form a cup shape.
7. Repeat with remaining pieces of cheese. Let cheese cups cool for 10 minutes.
8. Create salsa by mixing diced tomatoes, pepper, onion, lime juice and cilantro. Stir thoroughly and set aside.
9. Add taco ingredients to cheese cups. Top with salsa and serve.

Meatloaf

Serves: 6
Preparation time: 10 minutes
Bake time: 60 minutes

Ingredients:

Meatloaf:

- 2 lbs. ground beef
- 2 eggs
- ¼ cup onion, diced
- 2 garlic cloves, minced
- 1 tsp. coconut aminos

Sauce:

- 1 ½ cup mushrooms, chopped finely
- 2 Tbsp. tomato paste
- 4 oz. almond milk
- 1/3 cup almond flour
- 1 Tbsp. oregano
- 1 Tbsp. parsley
- Salt and pepper, to taste

Instructions:

1. Heat oven to 350 degrees (F).
2. Take ground beef out of the refrigerator and allow it to come to room temperature. This will help when mixing the meatloaf.
3. Add ground beef, eggs, onion, garlic, and coconut aminos in a large bowl. Use your hands to mix thoroughly.
4. Take a loaf pan and grease lightly.
5. Add meatloaf ingredients to the pan.
6. Next, combine the rest of the ingredients in a medium saucepan. Cook over low heat, and simmer for 2 minutes, stirring frequently.
7. Remove from heat.
8. Pour this sauce over the meatloaf.
9. Take loaf pan and put it in the oven. Cook until the meatloaf is done, about 50 to 55 minutes.
10. Remove from oven and let rest for 10 minutes before serving.

Beef Stroganoff Burgers

Serves: 5
Preparation time: 10 minutes
Bake time: 20-25 minutes

Ingredients:

- 1 lb. ground beef
- ¾ lb. ground turkey
- ¼ cup parsley, chopped
- 3 Tbsp. Worcestershire sauce
- 4 cloves of garlic, minced, divided
- 2 tsp. onion powder
- 1 ½ tsp. garlic salt
- Salt and pepper, to taste
- 3 Tbsp. butter
- 2 Tbsp. olive oil
- 3 Tbsp. cooking sherry
- ¼ cup yellow onion, diced
- ½ cup cremini mushrooms, sliced
- 1 ¼ cup beef stock
- 2 Tbsp. beef bouillon granules
- 1 cup sour cream
- 1/3 cup heavy cream

Instructions:

1. Combine ground beef and turkey in a large mixing bowl.
2. Add parsley, Worchester sauce, 1 clove of garlic, onion power, garlic salt, salt and pepper. Mix thoroughly. Form into 5 patties.
3. In large frying pan, sear the patties over medium high heat. Brown each side, about 2 or 3 minutes on each side.
4. Remove patties. They will not be fully cooked at this point
5. In the same pan, add butter, oil and cooking sherry. Heat ingredients over medium low heat.
6. Add onion, mushrooms and the rest of the garlic. Sauté mixture until the onions are opaque and the mushrooms tender.
7. Next, deglaze pan with beef stock, using a rubber spatula to scrape and incorporate garlic and onion that may have been stuck to the bottom of the pan.
8. Add beef granules, stir until dissolved.
9. Add sour cream and heavy cream, mixing into sauce.
10. Return patties to the frying pan and let them simmer in the cream sauce. Do not cover the pan.
11. Cook on low for 10 minutes and serve.

Low Carb Cheeseburger & Cauliflower Casserole

Serves: 8- 10
Preparation time: 15 minutes
Bake time: 30 minutes

Ingredients:
- 2 ½ cup cauliflower, chopped
- 1 ¼ lbs. ground beef
- 1 Tbsp. steak seasoning
- 5 oz. cream cheese, cubed
- 2/3 cup cheddar cheese, shredded
- 2 eggs
- 2/3 cup heavy cream or whipping cream
- 1 Tbsp. butter, melted

Instructions:
1. Heat oven to 400 degrees (F).
2. Add cauliflower to microwave safe bowl, microwave for 5 minutes.
3. While that is cooking, add ground beef to a frying pan and sprinkle steak seasoning over it.
4. Once the beef is sufficiently brown, add cauliflower, cream cheese and ¼ cup of the cheddar cheese.
5. Mix well. When fully incorporated, pour in a greased baking dish. Set aside.
6. In another bowl, scramble eggs with cream and butter.
7. Pour egg mixture over the beef. Top with the last ½ cup of cheddar cheese.
8. Put in oven and bake for about a half hour.
9. Remove from oven. Let set for 5 minutes and serve.

Slow Cooked Lamb

Serves: 6
Preparation time: 15 minutes
Bake time: 8 hours

Ingredients:

- 2 lbs. leg of lamb
- 1/3 cup olive oil
- 4 tsp. maple syrup
- 3 Tbsp. mustard
- 1 Tbsp. garlic powder
- Sea salt and pepper, to taste
- 1 Tbsp. dried rosemary
- 2 garlic cloves, sliced or minced
- 4 sprigs of thyme
- 7 mint leaves

Instructions:

1. Remove butchers string and any other netting from the lamb leg. Cut three slits into the meat.
2. Add to crockpot, rubbing with olive oil, syrup, mustard, garlic powder, salt and pepper.
3. Pack each slit with garlic and rosemary.
4. Cook leg of lamb in crockpot for 7 hours on low.
5. Remove lid. Add thyme and mint and cook for one more hour.
6. Let leg of lamb sit for 5 minutes, then slice and serve.

Keto Lamb Chops with Herbs Butter

Serves: 4
Preparation time: 6 minutes
Bake time: 12 minutes

Ingredients:
- 8 lamb chops
- Salt and pepper, to taste
- 2 Tbsp. butter
- 3 tsp. olive oil
- ½ cup herb butter
- 1 lemon, cut into wedges

Instructions:
1. Bring the lamb chops to room temperature. If the meat is cold when it is cooked, it won't brown as nicely. Also, slice a few cuts in the fat part, and the lamb chop won't curl when it's being cooked.
2. Sprinkle salt and pepper on the chops.
3. Add butter and olive oil to a frying pan.
4. When hot, fry each chop for 3 to 4 minutes. Thicker chops will need to cook longer, but it is okay if the lamb is a little pink on the inside.
5. Remove chops from heat. Add lemon wedges and serve with herb butter.

Easy Breaded Pork Chops

Serves: 4
Preparation time: 15 minutes
Bake time: 15 minutes

Ingredients:

- 4 center cut pork chops, boneless
- Sea salt and pepper, to taste
- 1 egg
- 1 Tbsp. water
- 2/3 cup Parmesan cheese, grated
- 2/3 cup pork rinds, crushed
- 2 Tbsp. garlic powder
- 2 Tbsp. parsley, minced
- 1 tsp. lemon zest
- 2 Tbsp. olive oil

Instructions:

1. Before you start, take the pork chops from the refrigerator and allow them to come to room temperature for about a half hour before you start cooking. It's important that the meat isn't overly cold when you bread them.
2. With a paper towel, dry the excess moisture, then season with salt and pepper.
3. Next, combine the egg and water, scrambling it thoroughly.
4. Make the low carb coating by combining the Parmesan cheese and pork rinds in a plate. If the pork rinds are too large, crush them a little more before moving forward.
5. Once the cheese and pork rinds are well incorporated, add the garlic and parsley; stir well.
6. Finally, zest the lemon and mix the zest in with the rest of the coating mixture.
7. Bathe the pork chop in the egg and water mixture. Make sure it's fully covered, but let the excess egg run off by holding it with a fork above the bowl.
8. Take the chop and coat it with the crumb mixture, pushing the pork chop gently into the coating to make sure it is well coated.
9. Set the pork chop aside and repeat the process.
10. Heat a large cast iron frying pan over medium heat and add your oil to the pan.
11. Once the oil is hot, add the pork chops to the pan.

12. Let them cook for about 5 minutes, and then flip them. Don't flip too quickly or the nice crust you constructed might start flaking off. Instead, make sure the bottom of the pork chop has a nice brown coating to it before you flip it.
13. Fry for another 5 minutes or so, or until done.
14. Remove from heat and let them rest for 8 to 10 minutes before serving

Parmesan Encrusted Pork Chops

Serves: 4-6
Preparation time: 10 minutes
Bake time: 12 minutes

Ingredients:

- 12-14 pork chops, boneless or bone in
- Salt and pepper, to taste
- ¾ cup Parmesan cheese
- 1 cup almond flour
- 1 Tbsp. garlic powder
- 3 eggs
- 1 Tbsp. water
- Bacon grease, ghee or olive oil for frying

Instructions:

1. Remove the pork chops from the refrigerator and let them come up to room temperature for about 20 to 30 minutes before starting to cook.
2. Preheat oven to 400 degrees (F).
3. When the chops are ready and seasoned with salt and pepper, finely grate the Parmesan cheese and mix it in with the almond flour and garlic powder.
4. Combine the egg with the water and scramble thoroughly.
5. Put the pork chops in the egg, coating them thoroughly but letting the excess egg mixture drop off.
6. Gently press the pork chop into the cheese mixture, coating it on both sides.
7. While the pork chops are resting, heat a frying pan with 2 Tbsp. bacon grease or an oil equivalent.
8. When the oil is hot, cook the pork chops in the oil for 1 minute.
9. Flip and cook the other side for an additional minute. The chops are sealed but not cooked at this time.
10. Put the pork chops on a parchment lined baking sheet and bake for about 10 minutes. The baking time will vary, depending on how thick the meat is.
11. When done, remove from oven and let rest for about 5 minutes before serving.

Instant Pot Smothered Pork Chops

Serves: 6
Preparation time: 10 minutes
Bake time: 45 minutes

Ingredients:

- 8 boneless pork loin chops, about 4 to 6 oz each
- 1 Tbsp. garlic salt
- 4 tsp. paprika
- 2 tsp. onion powder
- 1 tsp. pepper
- ½ tsp. cayenne pepper (more or less, depending on your desired level of spice)
- 3 Tbsp. coconut oil
- ¼ cup onion, diced.
- ½ cup baby portabella mushrooms, sliced

Gravy Sauce:

- 2 Tbsp. butter
- 2/3 cup heavy cream or whipping cream
- ½ tsp. xanthan gum
- 2 Tbsp. parsley, optional

Instructions:

1. Combine the garlic salt, paprika, onion powder, black pepper and cayenne pepper together. Mix well and set aside.
2. Next, rinse the pork chops under water and use a paper towel to pat them dry.
3. Sprinkle the spice mixture on both sides, gently rubbing the garlic mixture into the meat. Set aside the unused spices.
4. Next, turn your Instant Pot on to the sauté setting and add the coconut oil, letting it melt and heat.
5. Add the pork chops, a few at a time, browning them in the oil for 3 minutes. Flip and cook the other side for an additional 3 minutes.
6. Put the browned pork chops on a plate and set aside, repeating until all the pork chops are cooked.
7. Turn off the Instant Pot for the time being.
8. Add the sliced onions to the bottom of the pot and layer the sliced mushrooms on top of the onions. Lay the pork chops on top of the mushroom layer.
9. Close the Instant Pot and make sure the vent is closed off. Use the manual setting to cook the pork chops on high pressure for 23 to 25 minutes.

10. When cooking time is complete, let the pressure drop (either manually or letting it naturally drop) and remove the lid.
11. Plate the pork chops and set aside, either on the counter or in a warm oven.
12. Turn the Instant Pot to the sauté setting once more and, using a silicone whisk, combine the remaining spice mixture with butter and heavy cream.
13. Once well combined, sprinkle the xanthan gum into the liquid, whisking constantly.
14. Next, let the gravy simmer for 4 or 5 minutes until the sauce begins to thicken. If the gravy is not thick enough for your preference, add a little more xanthan gum, but note that the gravy will continue to thicken as it cools.
15. When the gravy is complete, top the pork chops with the gravy and, if desired, sprinkle with parsley. Serve.

Keto Flipped Pork Belly

Serves: 4
Preparation time: 45 minutes
Bake time: 2 hr, 15 minutes

Ingredients:

- About 2 ½ lbs. pork belly, raw
- 3 Tbsp. ghee or olive oil (you can also use lard, goose fat or duck fat)
- 2 Tbsp. sea salt
- 1 onion, large
- About ½ to ¾ cup fresh sage

Instructions:

1. Heat oven to 375 degrees (F).
2. Fill a pot of water and put it on the stove on medium high heat. Bring it to a rolling boil.
3. At the same time, make slits to the skin of the pork belly, but make sure you don't cut down to the flesh.
4. Put the pork belly in a bowl, skin side down and pour the boiling water over the pork belly. This opens up the skin a little more.
5. Carefully remove pork from the bowl and put it a baking tray, skin side up. At this point, take paper towels and pat the skin dry, getting it as dry as possible.
6. Next, rub your oil into the skin, making sure it goes into the slits as well. Take the salt and carefully rub that into the pork skin.
7. Flip the pork belly over so it's skin side down. Put it in the oven and roast for about 55 minutes to one hour.
8. Once roasting is done, remove the roasting pan from the oven and put the pork belly out of the dish, putting it on a plate for now.
9. Turn the temperature in the oven up to about 425 degrees.
10. Next, slice your onion into four rounds, placing them on the bottom of the roasting tray so they serve as a bit of a platform. Add sage leaves to the tray.
11. Now, turn the pork belly over once more so it's skin on the top again. Carefully place the pork on top of the onions.
12. Return to the oven and roast for another half hour until the skin is crisp and the internal temperature reaches 145 degrees.
13. Let it set for 5 minutes or so, and then serve.

Creamy Parmesan Garlic Pork Chops

Serves: 6
Preparation time: 10 minutes
Bake time: 20 minutes

Ingredients:

- 1 ½ lbs. boneless pork loin, cut into six pork chops
- 1/3 cup onion, sliced
- 2 to 3 garlic cloves
- 3 Tbsp. olive oil
- 1 ¼ cup heavy cream or whipping cream
- 2 oz. cream cheese
- ½ cup chicken broth
- ½ cup cheddar cheese
- 1 Tbsp. Italian seasonings
- Salt and pepper, to taste

Instructions:

1. Heat a cast iron frying pan, adding the oil and heating it.
2. Brown the pork chops, onion and garlic cloves at the same time. The pork chops should be cooked for about 4 or 5 minutes on one side, then flipped over and cooked on the other side.
3. When cooked, remove the pork chops from the pan and set them aside.
4. Put the remaining ingredients in the pan, and cook it on a medium heat until the sauce begins to thicken, using a whisk and stirring constantly.
5. When the sauce is thickened, return the pork chops to the pan and simmer on low heat.
6. Cook for an additional 5 minutes or until the internal temperature reaches 145 degrees.
7. Plate the pork chops and drizzle with sauce. Serve.

Vegetables

Sriracha Broccoli Salad

Serves: 5
Preparation time: 15 minutes
Rest time: 2 hours

Ingredients:

- 8 slices of bacon
- 1 ½ heads of broccoli (enough to chop into 4 cups)
- 1 red bell pepper
- 1 ¼ cup mayonnaise
- 2/3 cup cheddar cheese, shredded
- 1/3 cup sunflower seeds, dry roasted
- 2 tsp. apple cider vinegar
- 5 tsp. sriracha sauce
- Salt and pepper, to taste

Instructions:

1. Cook the bacon until it has reached your desired level of doneness. Let it cool on paper towels.
2. Meanwhile, cut the broccoli into bite sized pieces.
3. Dice the red pepper.
4. Crumble the bacon.
5. In a large bowl, add all the ingredients together and combine thoroughly.
6. When mixed properly, place in an airtight container and let it sit for a minimum of 2 hours to let the flavors incorporate together.

Big Mac Salad

Serves: 7
Preparation time: 10 minutes
Bake time: 10 minutes

Ingredients:

For the salad:

- 1 ¼ lbs. ground beef, or mixture of beef and turkey
- ¼ onion
- Sea salt and pepper, to taste
- 2/3 cup romaine lettuce, chopped
- 1 ¼ cup tomatoes, chopped
- 1 cup cheddar cheese
- ½ cup dill pickle spears

For the dressing:

- 2/3 cup mayonnaise
- 1 dill pickle spear
- 1 Tbsp. mustard
- 1 tsp. vinegar
- 4 ½ Tbsp. smoked paprika
- 2 Tbsp. sweetener, depending on taste

Instructions:

1. Heat skillet over high heat. Add ground beef and onion. Season with salt and pepper. Brown the beef, using a wooden spoon to break the pieces down. Fry for 7 to 10 minutes.
2. Add the dressing ingredients to your blender, and blend thoroughly. If it's too thick, add 1 tablespoon of water and blend again. Set the dressing aside in the refrigerator until ready to serve the salad.
3. Thoroughly mix the salad ingredients with the cooked ground beef. When you are ready to eat, toss with dressing and serve.

Cobb Salad

Serves: 1
Preparation time: 15 minutes
Bake time: 15 minutes

Ingredients:
- 3 slices bacon
- 1-2 romaine lettuce leaves
- 2 Tbsp. olive oil
- 1 Tbsp. apple cider vinegar
- Salt and pepper, to taste
- 1 avocado
- 1 red bell pepper
- 1 green onion
- 2 radishes
- 1 oz. bleu cheese, crumbled
- 1 egg, hard boiled

Instructions:
1. Heat a skillet and fry the three slices of bacon. When cooked set aside on paper towels to drain the extra fat.
2. When cooled, crumble the bacon.
3. Tear the romaine lettuce into bite sized pieces and toss it with the oil, vinegar and a pinch of salt and pepper. Place lettuce on a plate.
4. Prepare the avocado, bell pepper and onion by slicing into thin pieces.
5. Cut the radish into quarters and crumble the bleu cheese.
6. Remove shell from the egg and slice it.
7. Arrange the ingredients on the plated lettuce and serve.

Onion Soup

Serves: 7-8
Preparation time: 10 minutes
Bake time: 1 hour

Ingredients:

- ¼ cup ghee
- 5 onions, large
- 2 ½ cup chicken bone broth
- 1 ½ cup beef bone broth
- 6 garlic cloves
- Salt and pepper, to taste
- 8 oz. Swiss cheese, sliced (if desired)

Instructions:

1. In a stock pot or Dutch oven, melt ghee.
2. Thinly slice the onions and add to the pot. Cook over medium heat until the onions are brown and beginning to caramelize.
3. Add chicken broth, beef broth and garlic. Add salt and pepper to reach desired taste.
4. Bring soup to a boil. Reduce the temperature and simmer for 45 to 40 minutes, keeping in mind that the longer the soup simmers, the stronger the flavor will become.
5. If preferred, ladle the soup into ovenproof bowls or crocks.
6. Top with Swiss cheese and put under a low broiler setting to melt the cheese. Serve

Melitzanosalata (Greek Eggplant Salad)

Serves: 6
Preparation time: 15 minutes
Bake time: 1 – 1 ½ hours

Ingredients:

- 4 eggplant, medium sized
- Juice of 1 large onion
- Juice of 1 lemon
- 4 cloves of garlic, mashed
- ¼ cup parsley, chopped
- 1/3 cup olive oil
- Salt and pepper, to taste

Instructions:

1. Heat oven to 350 degrees (F).
2. Carefully wash and dry eggplants, being careful not to cut or piece the skins.
3. Place eggplants on a baking sheet lined with parchment paper.
4. Bake eggplant for 45 minutes to an hour, or until it is soft.
5. Once cooked thoroughly, remove from oven and allow it to cool.
6. To juice the onion, peel and chop the onion. Put it in a food processor and pulse until it is finely chopped. Put the chopped onion in cheesecloth and squeeze out the juice into a bowl.
7. Mix onion juice with the olive oil and lemon juice. Then add the garlic and parsley and mix well again.
8. Slice the cool eggplant and scoop out the flesh, putting it in a large bowl. Use a fork or potato masher to mash the eggplant, but don't break it down too far.
9. Add the herbs and oil mixture to the eggplant and mix well, seasoning with salt and pepper as desired.
10. Serve immediately.

Roasted Red Pepper Soup

Serves: 4
Preparation time: 10 minutes
Bake time: 20 minutes

Ingredients:

- 2 Tbsp. ghee or coconut oil
- 1 shallot, large
- 2 roasted red peppers, chopped
- 1 tsp. celery seed
- 4 tsp. seasoned salt
- 2 tsp. paprika
- ¼- ½ tsp. crushed red pepper flakes
- 2 heads of cauliflower (broken to 5 cups of florets)
- 4 ½ cup Chicken bone broth or vegetable stock
- 1 tsp. apple cider vinegar
- ¼ tsp. thyme
- 1 ¼ cup canned coconut milk

Instructions:

1. In a large heavy pot or a Dutch oven, heat coconut oil or ghee.
2. Chop shallot and add to the pot, cooking for about 3 minutes or until soft and opaque.
3. Add the red pepper with the celery seed, seasoned salt, paprika and red pepper flakes. Combine thoroughly and cook for an additional 2 to 3 minutes.
4. Next, add the cauliflower florets, chicken bone broth or vegetable stock, vinegar and thyme.
5. On medium heat, bring to a simmer. When at a gentle simmer, cover the pot and cook for 10 to 15 more minutes. The soup will be done when the cauliflower is soft and falling part.
6. Take small batches of soup and puree in the blender until all the soup is processed. Be careful, as the soup will still be very hot.
7. Once fully blended, put the soup back in the large pot. If it has cooled too much at this point, bring it back to temperature.
8. Once at its desired temperature, turn off the heat, mix in the coconut milk and serve

Sour Cream and Chive Broccoli Mash

Serves: 4
Preparation time: 5 minutes
Bake time: 10 minutes

Ingredients:

- 2 heads of broccoli
- 1 Tbsp. butter
- 3-4 oz. sour cream
- 3 Tbsp. chives, chopped finely
- Salt and pepper, to taste

Instructions:

1. Add 5 cups of water to a large pot. Place it on the stovetop over medium high heat and bring to a boil.
2. Chop the broccoli into bite sized florets, at a consistent size.
3. Place broccoli in boiling water. Cook for 4 to 5 minutes, until the broccoli becomes tender.
4. Remove the broccoli from heat. Drain it and then put it back in the warm pot.
5. Add the rest of the ingredients. Using a stick blender blend until there are no lumps.
6. Once at its desired consistency, stir in the chives and add salt and pepper to taste.

Crustless Keto Tomato Pie

Serves: 4
Preparation time: 10 minutes
Bake time: 30-35 minutes

Ingredients:

- 6 large tomatoes
- 2 tsp. olive oil
- 1 onion
- ½ cup herb blend of your choice (recommended: basil, tarragon, rosemary, sage and/or oregano)
- 2 cloves garlic, minced
- 16 oz. cheese, shredded (recommended: cheddar, Swiss, mozzarella, Monterey jack or smoked gouda)
- 1 ¼ cup mayonnaise
- Salt and pepper, to taste

Instructions:

1. Heat oven to 350 degrees (F).
2. Place a strainer in your sink or in a large bowl.
3. Slice tomatoes, sprinkling with salt. Place in the strainer and let them sit and drain for about 10 minutes.
4. Heat oil in a sauté pan and heat over medium heat.
5. Slice the onion into even sized pieces and add to the oil, stirring occasionally, for about 3 minutes.
6. While cooking, prepare the herbs and garlic. Add to the onions and cook for an additional 2 to 3 minutes. Remove from heat.
7. Stir cheese with mayo in a bowl and add in the onion mixture, stir well, adding salt and pepper to taste.
8. Spray a 9x13 casserole dish with cooking spray or rub it down with olive oil.
9. Line bottom of dish with one layer of tomato slices.
10. Next, layer, half of the cheese and mayonnaise mixture.
11. Layer the remaining tomatoes on that, the top with the remaining cheese mixture.
12. Bake for 30-35 minutes, or until the cheese on the top is slightly browned.
13. Scoop onto plates and serve.

Vegetable Bake with Creamy Pesto

Serves: 4
Preparation time: 30 minutes
Bake time: 35 minutes

Ingredients:
- 1 medium zucchini
- 1 red bell pepper
- 1 broccoli head
- ¾ red onion
- Salt and pepper, to taste
- Fresh basil leaves, for garnish

For Sauce:
- 2/3 cup pesto
- 2/3 cup heavy cream
- ¼ cup Parmesan cheese

Instructions:
1. Heat oven to 350 degrees (F).
2. Cut zucchini, red pepper and broccoli into large chunks.
3. Next, slice the onion into wedges, then separate the layers.
4. Toss the vegetables together with a pinch of salt and pepper.
5. Grease a 9x9 inch baking dish, and place vegetables in dish.
6. Bake for 30-35 minutes.
7. Meanwhile, mix together the sauce ingredients.
8. Remove from oven and serve with sauce and basil as garnish.

Garlic Baked Asparagus

Serves: 5
Preparation time: 5 minutes
Bake time: 20 minutes

Ingredients:
- 50 asparagus spears
- 1 Tbsp. olive oil
- 3 Tbsp. garlic salt
- 1 Tbsp. sea salt
- 2 ½ Tbsp. vegetable seasoning

Instructions:
1. Heat oven to 450 degrees (F).
2. Trim asparagus spears, and place in large bowl.
3. Toss with remaining ingredients.
4. Line a baking sheet with parchment paper.
5. Place prepared asparagus on sheet and put in the oven.
6. Bake for 10 minutes, then carefully flip the spears.
7. Cook for an additional 10 minutes.
8. Remove and serve.

Jalapeno Popper Cauliflower Casserole

Serves: 5
Preparation time: 15 minutes
Bake time: 20 minutes

Ingredients:

To make the puree:
- 1 cauliflower head
- 2 Tbsp. whipping cream
- 2 Tbsp. butter
- 2/3 cup cheddar cheese, shredded
- ½ tsp. garlic salt
- 1 jalapeno, seeds removed and chopped
- Salt and pepper, to taste

To make the cheese layer:
- 6-8 oz. cream cheese, softened
- 2/3 cup cheddar cheese, shredded
- 1/3 cup salsa verde

To make the jalapeno layer:
- 1 cup Colby jack cheese, shredded
- 3 jalapenos, seeds removed and sliced

Instructions:

1. Heat oven to 375 degrees (F).
2. First, clean and cut the cauliflower into even, medium sized pieces.
3. Place cauliflower in microwave safe bowl.
4. Add cream and butter to the bowl.
5. Microwave on high for 15-18 minutes, uncovered, stirring every 2-3 minutes to evenly cook. You may need to adjust cooking time, and remove once cauliflower is tender.
6. Take out of microwave and blend in a blender or food processer, along with the 2/3 cup cheddar cheese, garlic salt and 1 jalapeno.
7. Blend until a smooth consistency is reached.
8. Taste and add salt and pepper until the puree reaches the desired taste. Set aside.
9. Next, make the cream cheese layer. Pour cream cheese in microwave safe bowl and microwave for 25-35 seconds to soften. Add 2/3 cup cheddar cheese and salsa. Blend together thoroughly. The mixture should be very easy to spread. If it is not easily spreadable, microwave it for 5-10 seconds more until it is easy to spread.

10. Take square ovenproof dish and spray lightly with cooking spray. On the bottom of the dish, spread the layer of the cauliflower mixture.
11. Next, add the cream cheese layer.
12. On top of that, add the Colby jack and 3 sliced jalapenos.
13. Put the dish in the oven and bake for 18-20 minutes. If desired, finish under a low broiler for 2 minutes to brown the cheese.
14. Remove from oven and let set for 10 minutes before serving.
15. If desired, top with cooked bacon crumbles before serving.

Keto Creamed Spinach Soup

Serves: 3-4
Preparation time: 5 minutes
Bake time: 15 minutes

Ingredients:

- 2 ¼ cup water
- 2 lbs. spinach, uncooked
- 1 onion, large, diced
- ¾ tsp. garlic powder
- Salt and pepper, to taste
- ¼ stick of butter
- 2-3 oz. cream cheese
- 2 cup heavy cream

Instructions:

1. In a large pot, mix together the water, spinach, onion, garlic powder. Salt and pepper to taste. Bring to boil over medium high heat.
2. Once it reaches a boil, reduce heat and simmer the spinach mixture for 5-6 more minutes.
3. Remove from heat.
4. Carefully put spinach contents in blender or food processor and blend thoroughly.
5. Once smooth, return to the pot.
6. Add the rest of the ingredients and heat over medium heat for an additional 4 to 6 minutes. Serve.

Portabella Pizza

Serves: 5
Preparation time: 5 minutes
Bake time: 20 minutes

Ingredients:
- 5 portabella mushrooms
- 2 Tbsp. olive oil
- ½ onion, chopped
- 1 green pepper, chopped
- 1 or 2 garlic clove, minced
- Salt and pepper, to taste
- 2/3 cup pizza sauce
- 2/3 cup mozzarella cheese, shredded
- 3 Tbsp. Parmesan cheese, grated

Instructions:
1. Heat oven to 375 degrees.
2. Line baking sheet with parchment paper.
3. Prepare mushrooms by removing stems and place caps upside down on the baking sheet.
4. Bake in the oven for 9 to 10 minutes and take out of oven once ready.
5. Meanwhile, heat oil in cast iron frying pan over medium high heat.
6. Mix onion and green pepper in the skillet, cooking for 5 to 6 minutes. Stir frequently.
7. Next, add garlic, and salt and pepper to taste. Fry, stirring frequently, for 1 more minute.
8. Remove pan from heat.
9. If there is any excess moisture in the mushrooms, use paper towels to absorb the moisture.
10. In each mushroom, add 2 Tbsp. of pizza sauce, carefully spreading to edges.
11. Divide the pepper and onion mixture into 5 even portions and spoon each portion into the mushroom cap.
12. Place 2 Tbsp. of mozzarella and a 1 tsp. of Parmesan cheese on each mushroom.
13. Place the stuffed mushrooms back in the oven. Cook for an additional 9 to 10 minutes, or until the cheese is melted.

Mediterranean 'Pasta'

Serves: 4
Preparation time: 5 minutes
Bake time: 15-20 minutes

Ingredients:
- 3 Tbsp. olive oil
- 2-3 Tbsp. butter
- 1 cup spinach, raw
- 2 zucchini, large, spiral or thinly sliced
- 4-5 cloves garlic, minced
- Salt and pepper, to taste
- 2/3 cup sun dried tomatoes
- 2 Tbsp. capers
- 2-3 Tbsp. parsley, Italian flat leaf, chopped
- ½ cup Kalamata olives, cut in half
- 2/3 cup Parmesan cheese
- 2/3 cup feta cheese

Instructions:
1. Heat olive oil and butter in large cast iron frying pan over medium heat.
2. Add spinach, zucchini, garlic salt and pepper. Cook until the spinach is wilted and the zucchini is tender.
3. Remove from heat.
4. If there is excess liquid in the pan, drain liquid.
5. Add the rest of the ingredients to the pan, except for the cheeses.
6. Blend thoroughly and cook for an additional 2 to 3 minutes, stirring frequently.
7. Remove from heat and place in bowl. Toss with cheese and serve.

Creamy Low-Carb Red Gazpacho

Serves: 6
Preparation time: 10 minutes
Bake time: 30 minutes

Ingredients:

- 1 green pepper, large
- 1 red bell pepper, large
- ½ cup red onion
- 5 vine-ripened tomatoes
- 2 avocados
- 4 Tbsp. basil, chopped
- 2 Tbsp. parsley, chopped
- 2-3 garlic cloves
- 1 ¼ cup olive oil
- 3 Tbsp. apple cider vinegar
- 2 Tbsp. lemon juice
- Salt and pepper, to taste
- 1 European cucumber
- 2 green onions
- ¾ cup feta cheese

Instructions:

1. Heat oven to 400 degrees (F).
2. Line a baking sheet with parchment paper.
3. Half the peppers and remove core and seeds.
4. Place peppers, cut side down, on the baking sheet. Put it in the oven, roasting them for about 18-20 minutes, until the skin starts to blister and turn black.
5. Remove from oven and let cool.
6. In the meantime, prepare the red onion, chopping it in large pieces. Place in blender.
7. Once the peppers are cool, remove the skins and add to the blender.
8. Slice the tomatoes in quarters. Remove skin and seed from avocado, and add tomatoes and avocado to the blender with the onion.
9. Add herbs, garlic, olive oil, vinegar, lemon juice, salt and pepper. Pulse until the mixture is smooth.
10. Return to pot.
11. Cut the cucumber into small pieces and slice the green onions.
12. Add to pureed soup mixture and heat over medium heat, seasoning with salt and pepper to taste.
13. Serve with crumble feta cheese and fresh herbs. Leftovers can be refrigerated for as much as five days.

Keto Avocado Pie

Serves: 4
Preparation time: 25 minutes
Bake time: 40 minutes

Ingredients:

For the crust:
- ¾ cup almond flour
- ¼ cup coconut flour
- 3-4 Tbsp. sesame seeds
- 1 Tbsp. ground psyllim husk
- 1 tsp. baking powder
- Salt, to taste
- 4 Tbsp. olive oil
- 1 egg
- 3 Tbsp. water

For the filling:
- 2 avocados, ripe
- 1 ¼ cup mayonnaise
- 3 eggs, large
- 1 Tbsp. cilantro
- 1 chili pepper, chopped into small pieces
- ½ - ¾ tsp. onion powder
- Pinch salt
- ½ cup cream cheese
- 1 ½ cup cheddar cheese, shredded

Instructions:

1. Heat oven to 350 degrees (F).
2. In a food processor, combine flours, sesame seed, psyllium husk, baking powder, dash of salt olive oil, egg and water. Pulse until the dough forms a ball. This can also be kneaded together by hand, if necessary.
3. Line bottom of a springform pan with parchment paper. Grease the paper and pan side lightly with cooking spray.
4. Add dough to the pan and use your fingers to press dough on bottom and up the sides. Bake for 12-15 minutes.
5. Cut avocado in half, remove meat and dice.

6. Cut the chili in half and remove seeds and stem.
7. Combine avocado and chili in a bowl.
8. Mix in the rest of the ingredients.
9. Pour filling into prepared pie crust and return to oven.
10. Bake for 35-40 minutes, or until the top is a light brown.
11. Remove from heat and allow to sit for 5 minutes before serving.

Sides

Coconut Cauliflower 'Rice'

Serves: 6
Preparation time: 10 minutes
Bake time: 15 minutes

Ingredients:

- ½ head of cauliflower, 'riced'
- ¾ tsp. coconut oil
- 1 tsp. cardamom
- Pinch of coriander, optional
- 2/3 cup coconut milk, canned
- Salt and pepper, to taste

Instructions:

1. Cook and rice your cauliflower. (See "Cauliflower Fritters" recipe for instructions on how to rice cauliflower.)
2. Heat oil in large frying pan over medium temperature.
3. Add cauliflower. Cook for about 2 minutes until the cauliflower absorbs the oil.
4. Carefully add the rest of ingredients, and stir thoroughly to incorporate the flavors.
5. Stirring often, continue to simmer for 8 to 10 minutes. When the cauliflower is ready, it will be tender and the coconut milk will be absorbed into the mixture.
6. Add the remaining ingredients and stir thoroughly.
7. Simmer over medium heat for 5 - 10 minutes, stirring frequently, until the coconut milk is completely absorbed and the cauliflower is tender to your liking.

Creamy Caprese Cauliflower Casserole

Serves: 6
Preparation time: 10 minutes
Bake time: 1 hour 10 minutes

Ingredients:

- 1 cauliflower, cut into florets
- 1 ¼ cup tomato sauce
- 1-2 Tbsp. tomato paste
- ¼ cup whipping cream
- ½ cup Parmesan cheese, grated
- Red pepper flakes, optional
- Salt and pepper, to taste
- 8 oz. mozzarella, divided
- 1 1/3 cup grape tomatoes, cut in half
- ¼ cup basil, chopped

Instructions:

1. Heat oven to 425 degrees (F).
2. Set a baking rack in the middle of the oven.
3. Line a baking sheet with parchment paper.
4. Toss the cauliflower with 1 Tbsp. olive oil and salt and pepper.
5. Put on baking sheet and roast for 15 minutes.
6. Turn cauliflower over and roast for another 10-15 minutes, or until the cauliflower is tender.
7. Remove from oven and reduce the heat to 350 degrees (F).
8. Meanwhile, combine the tomato sauce and paste in a large saucepan. Heat over low heat.
9. When it's warm, add cream, Parmesan cheese, a pinch of red pepper flakes (if desired), and salt and pepper.
10. Remove the pot from the stove. Stir in the roasted cauliflower.
11. Next, carefully add half of the mozzarella, half the grape tomatoes and then a pinch of basil. Combine well.
12. Coat a baking dish with olive oil. Put the cauliflower into the baking dish. Place the rest of the cheese and tomatoes on the top.
13. Place in oven and bake for 25-30 minutes, then finish by broiling on low for an additional few minutes, until the cheese is bubbly.
14. Take the pan out of the oven and let it rest for about 5 minutes before plating.

Caprese Skewers

Serves: 2
Preparation time: 5-10 minutes

Ingredients:
- 16 oz. mozzarella cheese balls
- 2-3 Tbsp. pesto
- 2 pints cherry tomatoes
- ½ cup olives, mixed and pitted.
- 2 Tbsp. basil

Instructions:
1. Carefully combine the mozzarella with the pesto.
2. Make the skewers by alternatively piercing tomatoes, olives and cheese.
3. Serve with basil garnish.

Confetti Cole Slaw

Serves: 2
Preparation time: 10 minutes
Bake time: 10 minutes

Ingredients:
- 1 cup tri-colored coleslaw mix
- 1/8 cup red cabbage, shredded
- 1-2 green onion
- 2 radishes
- ¼ cup feta cheese
- 2 Tbsp. parsley, chopped
- 3 Tbsp. olive oil
- 3 Tbsp. apple cider vinegar
- Salt and pepper, to taste

Instructions:
1. Combine coleslaw mix, cabbage, feta and parsley.
2. In a separate bowl, mix the olive oil, vinegar and salt and pepper together.
3. Add vinegar mixture to the salad and toss.

Cauliflower Tater Tots

Yield: 50 tater tots
Preparation time: 30-40 minutes
Bake time: 15-20 minutes

Ingredients:

- 2 cup cauliflower florets
- 1 Tbsp. heavy or whipping cream
- 1 Tbsp. butter
- 1 Tbsp. ghee
- ½ cup cheddar cheese, shredded
- Salt and pepper, to taste
- 4 large egg whites
- Olive oil or ghee, for frying

Instructions:

1. Prepare the cauliflower florets and add to microwave safe bowl.
2. Add cream, butter and ghee and mix gently.
3. Microwave for 5 minutes on high, stirring after 3 minutes.
4. In a food processor, add the cauliflower mixture and cheese. Pulse until combined but still has small chunks.
5. Transfer the cauliflower in a bowl, add salt and pepper to taste and place in refrigerator for 30 minutes.
6. When the cauliflower is cooled, whip the egg whites until the eggs make stiff peaks in a mixing bowl.
7. Take about 1/3 of the egg and fold it into the cauliflower mixture. Mix carefully, adding more of egg white gradually until it is all gently mixed together.
8. Return to the refrigerator and chill for 30 more minutes.
9. Heat oven to 375 degrees (F).
10. Line cookie sheet with parchment paper.
11. Prepare a pastry bag with a round tube that has about a ¾ inch tip.
12. Spray bag with cooking spray and add cauliflower mixture.
13. Gently squeeze cauliflower onto baking sheet in inch long strips.
14. Cut with a butter knife for consistent 'tots'.
15. Bake for 11 to 12 minutes, until the mixture is puffy and a little brown. If you aren't finishing off by frying, bake for a few more minutes and serve immediately.
16. If opting to fry, heat about ¼ inch of oil in a cast iron frying pan. When it's hot, add the tater tots, frying for about 1 minute on each side. Serve immediately.

Parmesan Crisps

Serves: 12
Preparation time: 5 minutes
Bake time: 7-8 minutes

Ingredients:

- ¾ cup grated Parmesan cheese
- ¾ cup shaved Parmesan cheese

Instructions:

1. Heat oven to 375 degrees (F).
2. Line baking sheet with parchment paper.
3. First layer the bottom with ½ of the grated Parmesan cheese.
4. Add a layer of shaved Parmesan cheese then top with the rest of the grated Parmesan cheese.
5. Bake for 7-8 minutes.
6. Remove from oven and let cool for 3 minutes.
7. Using a pizza cutter, cut the warm cheese into 'chips'.
8. Cool completely and serve, or store in an airtight container.

Green Bean Casserole

Serves: 12
Preparation time: 15 minutes
Bake time: 35 minutes

Ingredients:

- ¼ cup onion, chopped
- 3 celery stalks, diced
- ½ mushrooms, sliced
- 4 cans green beans, either whole or French cut
- 1 ¼ cup heavy cream
- 1/3 cup mayonnaise
- Salt and pepper, to taste
- 1 cup Monterey jack cheese, shredded
- 1 cup cheddar cheese, shredded

Instructions:

1. Heat oven to 350 degrees (F).
2. Combine onion, celery and mushrooms.
3. Heat oil in a frying pan over medium heat and sauté the onion mixture until cooked.
4. In the meantime, lightly grease a casserole dish.
5. Drain green beans and put them in a bowl.
6. Mix in the cooked vegetables as well as the cream and mayonnaise. Stir to combine and add salt and pepper. Mix thoroughly.
7. Finally, add the cheese and combine well.
8. Place green bean mixture in the oven and bake for 35-40 minutes or until bubbly.
9. Remove and let sit for 5 minutes before serving.

'Potato' Salad

Serves: 6
Preparation time: 20 minutes
Bake time: 20 minutes

Ingredients:

- 6 eggs
- 1 turnip, diced
- 1 rutabaga, diced
- ¼ cup celery root, diced
- 1 Tbsp. peppercorns
- Salt, to taste
- 2 bay leaves
- ¼ cup onion, diced
- 3 dill pickle spears
- 2 Tbsp. apple cider vinegar
- 1 cup mayonnaise
- ½ - 1 tsp. Dijon mustard
- 1 tsp. celery salt
- 2 Tbsp. fresh parsley
- 2 Tbsp. fresh chives

Instructions:

1. Hard boil eggs and allow them to cool.
2. In the meantime, peel and dice the turnip, rutabaga and celery root into ¾ inch pieces.
3. Fill a large pot with water. Add peppercorns, salt and bay leaves.
4. Add the vegetables. Over a high heat, bring the water mixture to a rolling boil.
5. Reduce heat to medium and continue to simmer the contents for about 12-15 minutes, or until the rutabaga is tender.
6. Remove from heat and strain in a strainer.
7. Remove the spices and discard.
8. Place the vegetables in a bowl and allow it to cool.
9. Next, chop the onion and dice the pickles. Add to the cooked vegetables.
10. Remove the hard boiled eggs from the shells carefully. If they don't peel easily, try cracking and peeling just the top of the egg and then inserting a spoon to separate the egg from the shell, running the spoon around the entire shell to loosen up the egg before removing it.

11. Chop the egg and add to the vegetables mixture. Blend with vinegar.
12. Next, add the final ingredients, along with salt and pepper to taste. Mix until thoroughly combined.
13. For better results, refrigerate overnight in an airtight container before serving to allow all the flavors to blend.

Mexican Cauliflower Rice

Serves: 6
Preparation time: 10 minutes
Bake time: 5 minutes

Ingredients:

- 1 medium sized head of cauliflower
- 1 Tbsp. olive oil
- 2 Tbsp. ghee
- 2 cloves of garlic, chopped
- ¼ cup onion, chopped into fine pieces,
- 2-3 Tbsp. tomato paste
- Salt and pepper, to taste
- 2/3 cup chicken bone broth or vegetable broth

Instructions:

1. First, using either a handheld grater or the grating attachment a food processor, grate the cauliflower. Set aside.
2. Add oil and ghee to a large cast iron frying pain. Heat over high heat.
3. Add the garlic and onion and fry for about 2 to 3 minutes. The onion and garlic combination will be fragrant when ready and the onion will be soft.
4. Reduce heat to medium. Add the tomato paste and add salt and pepper to taste.
5. Next, add the grated cauliflower and the chicken or vegetable broth. Combine thoroughly. Cover the pot and let simmer for 3 to 4 minutes.
6. Remove from heat. If desired, use cilantro for garnish and serve.

Baked Parmesan Garlic Zucchini

Serves: 4
Preparation time: 55 minutes
Bake time: 20 minutes

Ingredients:

- 2 medium sized zucchinis
- 2 Tbsp. olive oil
- 2-3 Tbsp. minced garlic
- 2/3 cup Parmesan cheese, grated
- ¾ Tbsp. oregano
- Salt and pepper, to taste

Instructions:

1. Heat oven to 425 degrees (F).
2. Line the bottom of a cookie sheet with parchment paper.
3. Next, quarter the zucchini horizontally.
4. Place in a bowl and pour the olive oil and minced garlic over the zucchini.
5. Gently rub the zucchini with the garlic and olive oil to make sure all areas are thoroughly coated.
6. Place zucchini on prepared baking sheet, with the skin side down.
7. Next, sprinkle with the cheese and oregano, as well as salt and pepper to taste.
8. On the top rack of the oven, bake the zucchini for 15 minutes.
9. Carefully broil the zucchini for another 2 or 3 minutes, watching to make sure it doesn't burn.
10. Serve immediately. If you prefer, you can also sprinkle a little Parmesan cheese on the zucchini before serving.

Cauliflower Stuffing

Serves: 6
Preparation time: 15 minutes
Bake time: 30 minutes

Ingredients:

- ¼ cup butter or ghee
- ¼ cup onion, chopped
- ½ to 2/3 cup carrots, peeled and chopped
- 2 celery stocks, diced
- 1 small head of cauliflower, chopped into florets
- 1 cup white mushrooms, chopped
- Salt and pepper, to taste
- ¼ cup fresh parsley, chopped
- 3 Tbsp. rosemary
- 1 tsp. ground sage
- 2/3 cup chicken bone broth or vegetable broth

Instructions:

1. Melt butter or ghee in a large frying pan over medium heat.
2. Combine onion, carrot and celery in the pan and sauté for 7 to 8 minutes or until the vegetables are soft.
3. Next, add the cauliflower and mushrooms. Add salt and pepper as necessary.
4. Sauté the vegetables for an additional 10 minutes.
5. Finally, add herbs, stirring well until they are thoroughly incorporated.
6. Add broth, stir, and cover with a lid. Cook until the liquid is absorbed, and the vegetables are tender, 10-18 minutes. Serve.

Jalapeno Cornbread Mini Loaves

Serves: 8
Preparation time: 15 minutes
Bake time: 35 minutes

Ingredients:

- 1 2/3 cup almond flower
- 1 tsp. salt
- 2 tsp. baking powder
- ½ cup flaxseed meal
- 2/3 cup sour cream
- 3 Tbsp. butter or ghee
- 4 eggs
- 10 drops of liquid Stevia
- 1 tsp. Amoretti sweet corn extract (available in health food stores or online)
- 2/3 cup cheddar cheese, grated
- 2 jalapeno peppers, seeded and diced

Instructions:

1. Heat oven to 375 degrees (F).
2. Prepare a mini loaf pan (containing 8 loafs) by spraying it with a cooking spray.
3. In a large bowl, combine the almond flower, salt, baking powder and golden flaxseed meal.
4. In another bowl, combine the sour cream, butter or ghee, eggs, Stevia and sweet corn extract. Combine thoroughly.
5. Add the dry ingredients to the wet mixture and mix well, but do not overmix.
6. Next, fold in the diced pepper and cheddar cheese. Mix well.
7. Carefully spoon the batter into the mini loaf pan. If desired, top each loaf with a jalapeno pepper ring as garnish.
8. Bake for 20 to 23 minutes. The loaves will be done when they are a golden brown and the tops spring back to a light touch.
9. Remove the bread from the oven. Let the pan set for about 5 minutes before removing the mini loafs.
10. Place on a wire rack to cool completely before serving or storing in an airtight container.

Keto Coleslaw

Serves: 6
Preparation time: 15 minutes
Rest time: 14 hours

Ingredients:

- 2/3 cup mayonnaise
- 1 Tbsp. celery salt
- 2 Tbsp. apple cider vinegar
- ½ tsp. Steva
- Black pepper to taste
- 1 ½ cup coleslaw
- 1 spring onion, diced

Instructions:

1. Combine mayonnaise, celery salt, apple cider vinegar, Stevia and pepper in a large mixing bowl. Whisk to make sure it is combined well.
2. Next, add about half of the coleslaw mix, combining well, until the cabbage is well covered with the mayonnaise mix.
3. Then, add the remaining coleslaw mix. Combine well.
4. Add the chopped onions and mix again. Make sure all the cabbage and onions have a good coating of the mayonnaise mix.
5. Cover the salad and refrigerate for 2 hours.
6. Remove cover and stir. Return the cover and let refrigerate overnight, or for a minimum of 12 hours.

Grilled Eggplant Salad

Serves: 6
Preparation time: 10 minutes
Bake time: 20 minutes

Ingredients:
- 2-3 lbs. eggplant
- 2/3 cup olive oil
- 1/8 cup lemon juice
- 2 garlic cloves, minced
- 2/3 cup tomatoes
- 1 can tuna or 3 oz. anchovies
- ½ cup mozzarella cheese slices
- 4 Tbsp. mint
- Salt and pepper, to taste

Instructions:
1. Prepare grill or heat oven to 350 degrees (F).
2. Slice the eggplant into thick slices, lengthwise. Brush both sides with olive oil and sprinkle with salt.
3. Grill for 5 minutes or bake for 15 minutes, until the slices are soft. Turn after halfway cooking.
4. In the meantime, combine remaining olive oil, lemon juice and garlic. Set aside.
5. When the eggplant is cooked, remove from oven.
6. Pour the lemon juice mixture on the bottom of a plate or a platter, and set the baked eggplant in it.
7. After a minute or two, turn the slices so the other side can absorb the dressing.
8. Slice the tomatoes. Place on the platter, stirring a little so the dressing can coat it.
9. Top the eggplant slices with anchovies or tuna.
10. Take the sliced mozzarella, tear into pieces and arrange on top of the eggplant and tomatoes.
11. Finally, drizzle with a few tablespoons of olive oil and either lemon juice or apple cider vinegar.
12. Garnish with pepper and fresh mint and serve.

Easy Cheesy Zucchini Gratin

Serves: 6-7
Preparation time: 10 minutes
Bake time: 45 minutes

Ingredients:

- 3 cup zucchini, sliced, raw
- 1 onion, peeled and cut into thin strips
- 1 1/3 cup pepper jack cheese, shredded
- ¼ to 1-2 tsp. garlic powder
- 2 Tbsp. butter or ghee
- 1/3 – ½ cup heavy cream
- Salt and pepper, to taste

Instructions:

1. Heat oven to 375 degrees (F).
2. Prepare a square baking dish by lightly spraying with cooking spray or rubbing with olive oil.
3. Slice the zucchini. Take 1/3 of the zucchini and 1/3 of the onion slices and line the bottom of the dish.
4. Add a pinch of salt and pepper.
5. Top with ½ cup of cheese.
6. Repeat the layers two more times.
7. Next, mix together the garlic powder, butter or ghee and cream in a microwave safe dish. Microwave for about a minute, until the butter is melted. Stir.
8. Pour the mixture over the casserole slowly to let the liquid absorb into the dish.
9. Put the dish in the oven and bake for about 45 minutes. When ready, the top will be golden and the liquid thick.
10. Remove from oven and let set for about 5 minutes. Serve.

Conclusion

Starting a new diet is a daunting task. It takes time to learn what you can and cannot eat, while also learning how this new approach fits into your own life. However, by reading this guide, you have already taken a critical first step toward becoming a healthier you, healing your body and restoring your confidence, both in your physique and in the foods that you are eating.

As questions arise, there are a number of fantastic resources on the Internet to help keep you on the right track.

Happy healthy eating!

CPSIA information can be obtained
at www.ICGtesting.com
Printed in the USA
BVHW011039040419
544607BV00004B/435/P